IDEAS

&

ISSUES

Intermediate

Olivia Johnston
Mark Farrell

Chancerel

IDEAS & ISSUES
Intermediate

Editor Richard Larkham
Designer Valerie Sargent
Picture researcher Katharine Gasparini
Cover design Gregor Arthur

ISBN Book: 1 899888 24 1
Double Cassette Pack: 1 899888 25 X
Teacher's Guide: 1 899888 31 4
PN 6 5 4 3 2 / 04 03 02 01 00

Published by
Chancerel International Publishers Ltd
120 Long Acre
London WC2E 9PA
England

© Chancerel International Publishers Ltd 1998   **Printed in Hong Kong**

Text acknowledgements

The publishers and the authors would like to thank the following for
their kind permission to use extracts from copyright material:

- Carel Press for the article *How does this make you feel?* (p.6)
- Children's Express for *When a drink with dad turns kids into drunks* (p.34)
- The Daily Telegraph/Caldicot Censored Team for *Are today's teenagers victims of fashion?* (p.42)
- FHM magazine for *Slobbing is good for you* (p.90)
- Forbes magazine for *Pickled sheep and bullet holes* (p.14)
- Friends of the Earth for *Leave Your Car At Home!* (p.58)
- *The* **Guardian**/The Observer for *When a drink with dad turns kids into drunks* (p.34);
  Television exposure damages child speech (p.46); *Rich pickings, poor standards?* (p.62);
  Net addicts lead sad virtual lives (p.70); *Homeless are run out of town* (p.74)
- The Independent for *Arrest of black lecturer heightens distrust* (p.78)
- International Herald Tribune for *No Getting Around It: English Is Global Tongue* (p.66)
- Livewire magazine for *Brave new world?* (p.10)
- NATMAG Syndication for *The Concrete Ceiling* (p.86)
- New Woman magazine for *Real-life Couples* (p.38)
- Newsweek for *Children Of The Corn* (p.50)
- 19 Magazine for *I'm A Believer* (p.22)
- Solo Syndication for *Sex... Drugs... Alcohol? What really does go on in a teenager's bedroom?* (p.30)
- The Sunday Times for *The Ugly Duckling* (p.18) and *Teenage killers free after 5 months* (p.26)
- The Sydney Morning Herald and Paula Goodyer for *Diary of a walkout* (p.82)
- US News & World Report for *Living with a stranger* (p.54)

For information on some of the above publications, and Internet addresses, turn to **Sources**, pages 94 and 95.

IDEAS & ISSUES
Intermediate

Picture acknowledgements

The publishers would like to thank the following for permission to reproduce photographs:

Airwave (p.90-top left); All Action/Paul Smith (p.41); Laura Binetti (p.89); BT Corporate Picture Library (p.86); Chanel/Dominique Issermann (p.8-bottom right); Colorific! (p.20; John Moss, left; Steve Gardner/Black Star, centre; Tim Graham, right; Manny Millan/Sports Illustrated, p.93-bottom); Department of the Environment, Transport and Regions (p.35); Encyclopaedia Britannica International Ltd (p.73-left); Mark Farrell (p.38; p.39; p.46; p.61-bottom; p.56); Ford (p.72); Frank Spooner Pictures (Barros/Liaison, p.17-left; Alexis Duclos, p.20-bottom left; Kaku Kurita, p.23; Chiasson/Liaison, p.43-left; Gifford/Liaison, p.81); George Steinmetz/Katz Pictures Ltd (p.10-left; p.11-bottom); Goldcrest Films International Ltd (p.29); Caroline Haydon (p.12-top left; p,87); The Image Bank (p.76-right); The Independent/Tony Buckingham (p.78); Jan Chipps Photography (pp. 18; 19; 24; 25; 30; 32; 34; 40; 42; 44; 50; 52; 55-left; 57; 62; 63; 65; 68; 70; 72-left; 74; 75; 77; 80; 82; 83; 85-top; 88-a, c, e; 94; 95); Jay Jopling, London (p.14-right); League Against Cruel Sports (p.12-bottom); Liam Daniel/BFI Stills, Posters and Designs (p.48); Lisson Gallery/Mat Collishaw (p.14-left); Mary Evans Picture Library (p.31; p.33; p.55-right); Midnight Sun/Rune Stoltz Bertinussen (p.90-right); Modus Publicity (p.8-bottom left); Norman Tomlin/Bruce Coleman Inc (p.16-left); Ogilvy & Mather (p.59); Omega SA (p.92-left); One Little Indian Records (p.45-left); Oscar Faber (p.58); PA News (p.26; p.67-top); Parlophone/Paul Postle (p.45-right); People for the Ethical Treatment of Animals (p.10-right; p.11-top; p.51-right); Popperfoto (p.37); Private Eye (p.47; p.61); Punch (p.13; p.15; p.52; p.73-right); Red Rooster PR (p.43-right); Reflexion Photothèque (Sheila Naiman, p.67-bottom; Retna Pictures Ltd/Photographer (Ed Sirrs, p.84; Niels van Iperen, p.85-bottom; Michael Melia, p.92-right; Rocky Widner, p.93-top); Rex Features Ltd (p.21-left; E. J. Camp, p.21-right); Saatchi & Saatchi (p.8-top right); Scotland Against Drugs (p.36); Shilland & Co (p.9); Simons Palmer Agency (p.6); David Simson (p.12-top middle, centre left; p.64); Sony Computer Entertainment (p.71); Sporting Images Photo Library (p.91); Switzerland Tourism (p.90-bottom left); Sylvia Cordaiy Photo Library Ltd (John Peart, p.16-right and p.17-right; Guy Marks, p.20-bottom right; Mohira Smith, p.51-left; Christine Hipkiss, p.69; Graham Horner, p.88-b); Syriol Jones/19 Magazine/Robert Harding Syndication (p.22); Telegraph Colour Library (Paul Windsor, p,27; p.54-left; p.76-left); Tropix Photographic Library (D. Davis, p.12-centre right; D. Charlwood, p.20-top; Rolind Birley, p.54-right; R, Lane, p.60; M. & V. Birley, p.66); WSPA (p.12-top right).
The cartoon on page 49 is by Tom Lynham.
The chart on page 29 is based on information supplied by the Home Office. The chart on page 37 is based on information which appeared in *The* **Guardian**. The information in the chart on page 79 comes from the Labour Force Survey.

Every effort has been made to trace the copyright holders of material used in this book.
The publishers apologise for any omissions and will be pleased to make the necessary arrangements when *Ideas & Issues Intermediate* is reprinted.

CONTENTS

CONTENTS

5

1 Which recent advertisements can you remember? Why do you think you remember them?

Read about it

Peter is not like ordinary people.
He's done the marathon.

Just Do It

How does this make you feel?

TODAY, as part of a new advertising campaign from the sportswear giant, Nike, Peter Hull will appear on billboard posters all over London, alongside the slogan: "Peter is not like ordinary people…". Indeed he is not. Peter has no forearms and no legs and, we are told, he's done the London Marathon.

Peter hopes that his image will help to promote disabled sport. The cynical might say it will simply promote Nike. "I did wonder whether this ad was going to be in good taste," he admits. "But when they explained the idea to me, I quite liked it. It portrays me as an athlete, not a victim, and I think it's a positive message.

"The fact is, I've always been like this. I was born like this and you don't miss what you've never had. I dream of having limbs. Of course I do. But I'm happy the way I am and I get on."

Carel Press

2 Find the answers in the text to these questions.

a Which company is using Peter Hull in their advertisements?

b In what ways is Peter "not like ordinary people"?

c What does Peter hope the advertisement will promote?

d Why does he like the ad?

e How long has Peter been disabled? Does he seem depressed?

advertising campaign planned series of advertisements
giant extremely large company
billboard posters very big adverts at the side of the road
slogan advertising phrase that is easy to remember
London Marathon long-distance (41.8 km) race that takes place in London every year
promote make people more interested in
the cynical people who do not believe in human goodness
in good taste what most people think is artistically and socially acceptable; not offensive
portrays shows

Key Language

Read this sentence from the article.

> The cynical might say it will simply promote Nike.

We use **might** to say that something is a possibility. The negative is **might not** or **mightn't**.

Examples:
You might be right. = Perhaps you are right.
They might be lying. = Perhaps they are lying.
It mightn't work. = Perhaps it won't work.

3 Imagine you work at Nike's advertising agency. The Peter Hull advert is still at planning stage. Discuss it, using the prompts + *might/might not*.

a the campaign / not work
   The campaign might not work.
b a less shocking slogan / give a more positive message
c the message / not be very clear
d the ad / be exploiting his disability
e the ad / shock the public too much
f people / say the ad is not in good taste
g the ad / offend disabled people

4 Fill each gap with a word or phrase from the glossary.

a I don't like that ad because it ___ women as passive sex objects.
b Their ___ , *Real Juice For Real People*, is easy to remember.
c ___ can be more effective than TV commercials because so many people drive past them every day.
d An advertising agency looks at new ways to ___ the product.
e Then it launches an ___ in the press and on TV.

Talk about it

5 How do you know the Peter Hull photo is an advertisement for Nike?

6 What does the slogan *Just Do It* mean?

7 The advert does not tell us to buy Nike products. Why not?

8 Which three adjectives from this box best describe the ad? Discuss your choice with a partner.

absurd	clear	dishonest
humorous	interesting	modern
offensive	pointless	shocking
dramatic	striking	stylish
thought-provoking	ugly	touching

9 What do you think of the Nike ad? Give reasons for your opinion. These notes may help you:

- in good taste? / in bad taste?
- promotes disabled sport? / pretends to promote disabled sport?
- makes you admire Peter? / makes you feel sorry for him?
- good for Nike's image?
- will make people buy Nike products?

10 What do you think of advertising in general? Choose from the suggestions below or give your own ideas.

entertaining?   dishonest?
a type of art?   a waste of money?
a useful way of finding out about products?

ADVERTISING

ADVERTISING

Tune in

1 Before you listen, name one good thing and one bad thing about advertising.

2 Now listen to a radio discussion about advertising and note down the four opinions. Did you give any of these opinions in your answer to Question 1?

3 Listen again and complete the speakers' actual words.

a Angela: "ads make you buy things you don't need *and can't afford.*"
b Dave: "the best ads are works ____ ."
c Diane: "too many ads exploit ____ ."
d Angela: "a lot of ads make people feel ____ ."

ONE SIZE FITS ALL

4 In your opinion, which of these adverts, best illustrate(s) the opinions in Question 3?

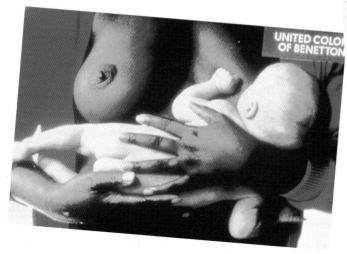
UNITED COLORS OF BENETTON

N° 5

Key Language

Here are some ways of giving or asking opinions.

Giving opinions
☐ *It seems to me...*
☐ *In my opinion...*
☐ *Personally, I think...*
☐ *My feeling is that...*
☐ *As I see it...*
☐ *If you ask me...*

Asking opinions
☐ *Do you agree that...*
☐ *We want your views on...*
☐ *How do you feel about...*
☐ *Where do you stand on...*
☐ *What do you feel about...*
☐ *What's your view on...*

5 Listen to the tape again and tick (✓) the phrases opposite, as you hear them.

6 In pairs, ask and answer opinions about:
- the adverts on this page
- any recent adverts that you can remember
- advertising in general

Over to you

7 How successful is this advertisement? Give your views in a one-minute speech.
Consider these points:

- What is the ad for and how do you know?
- Why are the jeans made of concrete? (The message?)
- How is colour used?
- Who is the advertisement aimed at: men, women or both?
- Will people remember the ad? Why/why not?

8 Guess the ending of the slogan which normally accompanies the ad:

LEVI'S® 505 ZIPFLY JEANS
a Make you feel like a statue!
b Worn by Construction Workers since the 1960s.
c Heavier than concrete.

Check with your teacher for the correct slogan. Which one do you think is best and why? Write another slogan to go with the picture.

9 Give a name to one of the following products and write a radio commercial for it, for two actors. Then act out the commercial to the rest of the class.

shampoo	paint	perfume
a chocolate bar	trainers	sports shoes
make-up	hi-fi	mobile phone

10 In Britain, the ASA (Advertising Standards Authority) controls advertising. Here are some of its rules:

- ❏ Advertisements must be "legal, decent, honest and truthful".
- ❏ There can be no TV or cinema advertising of cigarettes.
- ❏ Advertisements for alcoholic drinks should not be aimed at under-18s. They should not suggest that a drink will make a person more popular.
- ❏ Advertisements should not make children feel unpopular for not buying a product.

What do you think of the ASA rules? Is there an advertising authority in your country? Have you seen any adverts that break any of these rules? Make up two more rules.

Write about it

11 Describe in detail an advert you like very much.
Explain why you like it.

Write 50–100 words. Start like this:

I really like the ad for ___ which features...

12 Write a letter to the advertising standards authority in your country complaining about a recent ad which you found offensive. Describe the ad, say where you saw it and explain why you found it offensive. Write 50-100 words. Start:

Dear Sir or Madam,
I recently saw an advertisement for ___ which I found offensive. The advertisement was in/on ___ . It showed ___ . I found it offensive/shocking because...

1 What sort of experiments on animals do you know about? What is an animal rights activist?

Read about it

Brave new world?

Man has bred animals for research for decades, but their use in the laboratory is increasing. In 1994 the total number of experiments on animals rose by 15,000 to 2.8 million. Genetic manipulation of animals is now the fastest-growing area of vivisection. The number of creatures whose genes were tinkered with as part of an experiment, rose by 22 per cent to 256,000.

Brothers Charles and Jay Vacanti hope the technique they are pioneering, growing an ear from human cells on the back of a genetically-engineered mouse, could be used to reconstruct ears lost in accidents or to give normal hearing to children born without ears.

There are plenty of protesters queuing up to oppose these developments. "It's obscene," declared a spokeswoman for Compassion in World Farming. "Shocking and bizarre," added a senior researcher for the British Union for the Abolition of Vivisection.

Some organizations have taken their concern to the European Courts. The focus of this legal challenge is the so-called "onco-mouse", a rodent bred specifically to contract cancer so that the disease, and potential treatments, can be better understood. To animal rights activists, onco-mouse is an animal designed to suffer and die prematurely.

Livewire

2 Find the answers in the text to these questions.

a How many experiments on animals were done in 1994?

b What does the Vacanti brothers' research consist of?

c What is the aim of the research?

d List three adjectives used by protesters about this type of activity?

e What do scientists hope to learn from the "onco-mouse"?

bred animals kept animals (so that they produce baby animals)
vivisection operating on living animals for research
tinkered with changed, altered
pioneering developing for the first time
queuing up ready immediately
concern worry, anxiety
European Courts official tribunals which represent the European Union countries
focus principal area
challenge opposition
rodent small animal with long, sharp front teeth, eg. rat, mouse, rabbit.

Key Language

Read these sentences from the article.

> There are plenty of protesters queuing up...
> ... onco-mouse is an animal designed to suffer...

The sentences have the same meaning as: *There are plenty of protesters **who are** queuing up...*
*... onco-mouse is an animal **which is** designed to suffer...*

3 Replace the participles in *italics* in the sentences below with *who/which* + verb.

a The Vacantis hope to help children *born* without ears.

b They also hope to reconstruct ears *lost* in accidents.

c Scientists *experimenting* with animals get a lot of opposition.

d Onco-mouse is a rodent *bred* to contract cancer.

e Animal experiments are essential to scientists *looking* for new medicines.

f Most animals *living* in cages seem unhappy.

g People shouldn't buy products *tested* on animals.

4 In pairs, give your opinions about sentences **e**, **f** and **g** in Exercise 3.
Start like this: *I agree that... / I'm not convinced that... / I'm not sure if...*

Talk about it

5 Give some of the reasons why scientists do experiments on animals.

6 Do you think there is a difference between using animals for testing cosmetic products (eg. shampoo, skin creams) and using animals for testing medicines?

7 What is your reaction to this photo and the ones on the opposite page?

8 Could you ever do a job that involved animal experiments? Why/why not?

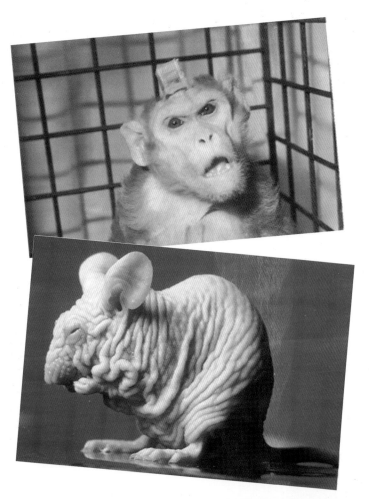

Tune in

1 Before you listen, make a list of activities which animal rights activists might be opposed to. Use the pictures on this page to give you some ideas.

2 Now listen to an animal rights activist talking. Which things in the pictures does she mention?

3 Listen again and answer these questions.

a How do foxhunters hunt the fox? On foot? In cars? On horses?
b What do they use – guns, traps or dogs?
c Why do animals sometimes bite off their own paws?
d Which animals are in danger of extinction because of poachers?
e Why do poachers kill these animals?

12

Key Language

4 Listen to the tape and complete the sentences with a gerund (an *-ing* word).

a I am opposed to ___.
b ___ animals for their fur is another terrible practice.
c ___ fur coats isn't glamorous.
d ___ face creams on rabbits is wrong.
e ___ monkeys into space with electric wires attached to their brains is immoral.
f ___ cruel to animals is bad for our own souls.

5 Make up four questions about animals that you would like to discuss. Use the gerund (*-ing*) in each question. Then ask and answer the questions.

Examples:
Do you think keeping animals in cages is cruel? Yes, I do. / I'm not sure. / It might be cruel but sometimes it's necessary.

Over to you

6 Look at the cartoon below. What is its message? Do you think it is funny? Why/why not?

7 What do you think of zoos? Describe your last visit to a zoo. What is good and what is bad about zoos?

8 Do you think it's right to use wild animals in circus shows? Is there a difference between training wild animals, and training dogs to work with blind people or the police?

9 Make a list of ways in which humans use animals. Should we use them in all these ways? Why/why not?

"As you can see we're very humane in the way we test cosmetics on animals"

Write about it

10 Write a letter to a company producing shampoo or cosmetics tested on animals. Explain why you are opposed to animal testing and try to persuade them to give it up. Start like this:

Dear ___ ,
I am concerned because I have heard that you test all your products on animals. You say that this makes the products safer to use. I do not agree because...

11 Imagine you are a scientist who uses animals for research. Some animal rights activists break into your laboratory, take away the animals and leave you a threatening note. Write a statement to the police. Start like this:

"I work in ___ Laboratory. I am a scientist, doing research on ___. When I went back to my laboratory after the weekend break, I found the place in chaos ... "

13

1 Have you been to an art exhibition recently? Was it sculpture, painting or something completely different – like the objects on this page? Did you enjoy it?

Pickled sheep and bullet holes

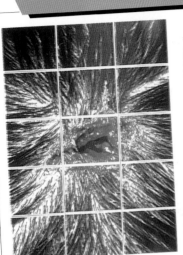

DEAD SHEEP, sharks and cows immersed in formaldehyde? A bullet wound on a human head?

Such "art" drives animal rights activists nuts and is a guaranteed turn-off for a lot of other people, but it has succeeded in drawing attention to young British sculptors and painters.

Attention is exactly what Damien Hirst, 29, ringleader of this new group of British artists, wants. He has developed his own method of selling his art, in the tradition of Andy Warhol. In 1988, he and some fellow student artists put together their own show, bypassing the established galleries.

One especially provocative piece by Hirst was a 14-foot shark preserved in a tank of bluish formaldehyde entitled "The Physical Impossibility of Death in the Mind of Someone Living". Hirst followed up with more pieces featuring dead animals – including a cow and a calf, sawn in half. Its title: "Mother and Child Divided".

Now Hirst and friends are coming to the U.S. The Walker Art Center in Minneapolis will stage a major exhibit in October – ""Brilliant": New Art from London"".

If you want to go and see Hirst's pickled sheep, it's currently on exhibit at the Chicago Museum of Contemporary Art. The piece was recently vandalized by enraged animal rights activists, but it has since been restored.

Forbes

2 Why is the word "art" (*paragraph 2*) in inverted commas?

3 What is the attitude of animal rights activists to Damien Hirst's work? What action did they take?

4 The title "Mother and Child Divided" is a sort of joke. Can you explain the joke?

5 Why do you think Damien Hirst wants attention?

pickled (usually food) kept in vinegar or other chemical to stay fresh
bullet you shoot bullets from a gun
immersed put in liquid
formaldehyde chemical for preserving dead animals in laboratories
wound damaged part of your body
drives nuts makes very angry
a turn-off something unpleasant
ringleader leader of a group of people
bypassing ignoring, avoiding
galleries places where you see art – a shop or a museum
provocative making people think and perhaps get angry
featuring including
calf young cow
sawn cut with a saw
exhibit (AmE) exhibition
enraged very angry

Key Language

6 Look at the words *artist*, *painter*, *sculptor*.
The word endings *-ist -er* and *-or* are often used to indicate people's jobs. You can make your own words with *-er* (but *-or* and *-ist* are less common). Make five job titles with *-er*.

7 Use these words to fill the gaps in the sentences.

- guitarist • psychiatrist
  - driver • author
- photographer • actor

a Ayrton Senna was a brilliant racing ___ .
b Who is the bass ___ in the band Oasis?
c My favourite ___ is Kevin Costner.
d The name of the ___ is usually on the cover of the book.
e With modern cameras, everyone can be a good ___ .
f I'm not mad. I don't need a ___ .

8 Complete these sentences, using words with *-er/-or/-ist*.

a If you're a top ___ , you want to win Wimbledon.
b I'm so ill that I can't move. Please call a ___ .
c My sister's a ___ . She writes for the *New York Times* newspaper.
d I'm studying psychology, but I don't want to be a ___ .
e We had a wonderful maths ___ at school. That's why I like it.
f I've been skiing for years, but I'm still not a good ___ .

9 Make sentences using the words below.

- director • professor
- runner • drummer • hunter
  - geologist • cleaner

Talk about it

10 Here are some strange works of art. You are a gallery guide. Give a short talk on one of them.

- A bathroom. You look into it through a hole in the door.
- Little bottles containing things from the artist's body – hair, skin etc.
- A bed covered with pages from the Bible.
- A broken television.
- A Christmas tree hanging upside down.
- A real homeless man standing by the wall in the art gallery.

11 Most of these strange works are trying to communicate ideas, rather than be "beautiful". They have a message.
Is this the right thing for art to do?

12 Janice Jeavons, a London art critic says: *"People have been making paintings and sculptures for thousands of years. You can't do anything new with them. It's time to experiment with new media."* Do you agree?

13 Should critics, or the public, tell artists what to do? Or should artists be completely free to do whatever they like?

A cartoonist's view on creating art!

14 Many famous artists from the past were considered strange and revolutionary in their time. Think of Pablo Picasso or Salvador Dalí. Do you think Damien Hirst will be famous 100 years from now?

15 What strange and original work of art would you like to do yourself?

 **Tune in**

1 Before you listen, look at the pictures of graffiti below and opposite
Is there graffiti where you live? Do you like it or hate it?

2 Now listen to Tony Sotelo, a graffiti artist in New York.
Is he proud of what he does, or does he feel like a criminal?

3 Here are some comments from people in New York.
Do you think Tony would agree or disagree with them?
Write **A** (agree) or **D** (disagree).

a *"Graffiti makes the town look better."*
b *"Doing graffiti can be dangerous."*
c *"Most graffiti artists are paid for their work."*
d *"Felt tip pens are just as good as spray cans."*
e *"The important thing is to write your 'tag' – your name –
   for everyone to see."*
f *"Graffiti artists have a better attitude than 'normal' painters."*

---

subway train (AmE) underground
   train
felt tip pen pen with a soft tip
tag graffiti artist's nickname,
   often strange (eg. "Fisto",
   "Zaki", "Elk", "Cal")
spray cans cans of paint with
   button to spray the paint
murals big paintings on walls

Key Language

The verb ***to get*** is used much more in spoken English than
in the written language. It has many uses.

Examples:
1 *Get a computer!* = Buy/Borrow a computer!
2 *He gets $20 an hour.* = He receives/is paid $20 an hour.
3 *I got on to graffiti.* = I started doing graffiti.
4 *They got to meet Wynona Ryder.* = They had the opportunity of meeting Wynona Ryder.
5 *She got arrested.* = She was arrested.

4 Listen to the tape again and complete these sentences.

a I got a big black ___ .
b Then I got on to ___ .
c Kids hide in tunnels and get ___ .
d We are not like the painters who get ___ .
e We don't get ___ .
f But everyone gets to ___ .

5 Now match the phrases **a-f** in Exercise 4 to the uses of *get* (**1-5**) in *Key Language*, eg. **b+3**.

Over to you

6 What do you think of the graffiti on these pages? Is it beautiful? Do think it is the work of *real* artists? Could *you* do it?

7 Do you agree with Tony Sotelo that graffiti is the art of the people, that it is "democratic"?

8 Roleplay this situation.
> An angry shopkeeper finds a graffiti artist spraying the side of the shop –
> not just a "tag", but a big, colourful mural. Instead of running away,
> the artist stays and argues with the shopkeeper.

Act out the parts of the artist and the shopkeeper.

9 A graffiti artist in Sheffield, England, was recently sent to prison for five years. The judge said it would cost £7000 to clean the walls he had painted. Do you feel that the punishment was right?

Write about it

10 A friend of yours is in trouble for doing graffiti on the wall of the school. Write a letter to the headteacher, defending your friend.

11 Write a magazine article with the title *Graffiti – the Art of the 21st Century*.

1 What makes a person beautiful? A perfect face? A good body? A healthy attitude to life? A good character?

2 There is a famous children's story called *The Ugly Duckling*. Do you know what happens? The article below has the same title. Can you guess what it is going to be about?

Read about it

The Ugly Duckling

I realised how cruel life can be for an unattractive child when everybody in my class was invited to a tenth birthday barbecue on the beach. Everybody, that is, except for me. At first I thought there had been a mistake and that my invitation had been lost. But when I made inquiries to the hostess, she didn't beat about the bush: "Sorry, Susie. You're too fat to wear a swimsuit on the beach and you can't see without those horrible glasses anyway."

I went home and cried for hours. My mother was ready with comforting cuddles, yet even she couldn't bring herself to reassure me I was lovely. I used to spend a long time staring at my brother and twin sisters and feeling extremely hard done by.

The chip that was developing on my shoulder became obvious in my aggressive manner. This, of course, only made things worse.

Tea invitations stopped, I walked home from school alone and often found drawings that looked like me in the classroom wastepaper bin. I hated everyone because everyone seemed to hate me.

When I was 14, my mother decided that I should go to the church youth club. I stood alone watching the dancing, feeling embarrassed, ugly and awkward. Then a miracle happened.

A skinny boy called Peter, with glasses and spots, asked me to dance. He also had a brace on his teeth. We didn't talk much but he asked if I would be there the following week. I have to credit Peter with changing my life. He stopped me feeling hideous.

Encouraged, I put myself on a diet, begged my mother for contact lenses and grew my hair. Then another miracle occurred. I grew taller and, as that happened, I started looking slimmer. The brace was finally removed and my teeth were even. I was never going to be a beautiful swan, but I was going to try.

THE SUNDAY TIMES

3 Find the answers in the text to these questions.

a Why wasn't the writer invited to the party?

b Why do you think Susie felt "hard done by" when she looked at her brother and sisters?

c How did the other children react when Susie became aggressive?

d What was the first "miracle" which increased Susie's self-confidence?

e What were the three ways in which Susie tried to improve her appearance?

beat about the bush waste time before saying something important
cuddles embraces
bring herself force herself
hard done by unfairly treated, unlucky
chip ... shoulder inferiority complex
tea early evening meal
awkward uncomfortable
skinny extremely thin
brace metal frame (for straightening teeth)
credit ... with be grateful to ... for
hideous very ugly
even straight

Key Language

Read this sentence from the article.

> I used to spend a long time staring at my brother...

Used to means something regularly happened in the past but doesn't now. The negative form is **didn't use to**. The interrogative form is **Did ... use to...?**.

Examples:
I used to wear glasses but I wear contact lenses now.
She didn't use to worry about her appearance when she was younger.
Did you use to wear a brace when you were a child?

4 How have you changed? Tell your partner about these topics.

• appearance   • sports and exercise   • food   • family

Make 10 statements with *used to/didn't use to*. Here are some examples:

I used to have long hair but now it's short.
I didn't use to do much exercise but now I play a lot of tennis.

Talk about it

5 Prepare to retell Susie's story in your own words. Write brief notes. Close your books. In groups tell the story, each person saying a sentence.

6 Do you think the girl was right to exclude Susie from her birthday party? Why/why not?

7 Which aspects of her appearance did Susie worry about most of all ? What other aspects do teenagers worry about? (Look at these photos.)

8 How do you choose your friends? What influences you in your choice? Put these ideas in order of importance (**1** = most important, **9** = least important) and discuss your decision with a partner.

sense of humour   physical appearance   money
taste in music/TV/films   dress sense
interests   personality   intelligence
similar education/family background

1 Before you listen, describe to a partner one of the beauty practices illustrated on this page. Use words from the box. Your partner has to guess which one you are describing.

> lower lip   ears/earlobes   neck   nose
> face   wooden plate   brass rings
> stick   pierce   stretch   decorate   paint
> scar/make scars (on)

2 You are going to hear a talk about beauty around the world. Which beauty practices shown in the pictures below does the person talk about?

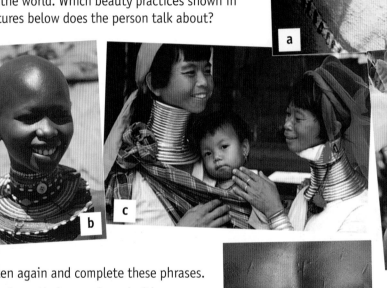

3 Listen again and complete these phrases.
a They have their ___ pierced with a sharp stick.
b They have a piece of wood ___ in the lip.
c Every month they ___ a larger piece of wood put in.
d Masai girls have their ears ___ with heavy weights.
e We ___ braces ___ our teeth.

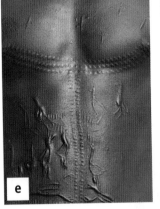

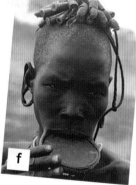

Key Language

Look at the sentences which you completed in Exercise 3. What type of verb construction is used?

We use **have/get something done** to say that we organise somebody to do something for us.

4 Ask and answer questions with *have/get* something done, using the prompts **a-i**.

Examples:
Have you ever had your hair dyed?
Would you ever get your nose pierced?

a ears pierced
b hair dyed
c hair shaved off
d nose/lip/tongue/eyebrow pierced
e a tattoo done
f legs waxed
g hair permed
h hair cut very short
i plastic surgery done

Over to you

5   Look back at the photos of beauty practices on the opposite page. Which woman is the most beautiful? Which image do you react most strongly to and why? Which practice do you find the most acceptable? Which practices do you think are bad for women?

6   Choose one of the following statements and prepare an argument to support it. (Don't worry if you don't believe in it!) Make some notes first.

"It's much more important for women to be attractive than for men."
"You don't have to be physically perfect to be attractive. You just have to be self-confident."
"Beauty contests are an insult to women."
"There are many disadvantages in being good-looking."
"To be beautiful, you have to suffer."

7   Roleplay a conversation between two people. One person has decided to have a tattoo done, the other is trying to persuade him/her not to. Use some of these ideas:

- tattoo where on the body?
- what type?
- need parents' permission (under 16)
- painful

- indelible
- looks good/tough/ fashionable/cool
- friend has tattoo
- don't mind the pain

8   When do you think plastic surgery is a good idea?

Gérard Depardieu refuses to change his nose

Cher has had plastic surgery on her nose and breasts

Write about it

9   You are a journalist who works on the problem page of a magazine. You receive a letter from someone who is worried about his/her appearance. Write a reply giving advice and encouragement. Start like this:

Dear ____ ,
First of all, let me tell you that you are not alone. Many people worry about some aspect of their appearance...

10 Describe your ideal partner. Talk about appearance and personality. Start:

"My ideal partner would be ____. He/She would have ... "

1 Can you name any religious cults? How did you hear about them and what do you know about them?

I'M A BELIEVER

Jane Allison joined the Unification Church – the Moonies – three days after her 18th birthday

"I met up with some girlfriends and someone suggested going to a Moonies meeting for a laugh. We went along and were surprised – everyone seemed kind and intelligent. I started going to their meetings and hanging out with them at weekends. They talked about helping the elderly and poor and working towards a better world. I told my parents about them but they told me to stop seeing them immediately. I'm not a rebellious person but I didn't see why I should stop – they knew nothing about it. Just after my 18th birthday the Moonies asked me if I wanted to join them officially in London. I said "yes". It seemed the right thing to do.

I went to a big house in Kent to do a 21-day workshop. By the end of the 21 days everybody feels euphoric.

But what was actually going on without me realizing it was a classic form of brainwashing.

I left to join a Moonie centre in Leeds. My life revolved around fundraising and trying to get new recruits. I got up at 8 am and didn't stop until 11 at night, seven days a week. I carried on like that for nearly four years. I hardly ever saw my family. They kept writing and phoning but I wasn't interested. I believed they were evil because they were trying to steal me away from the organisation.

One day I couldn't take any more and when everyone was out I rang a friend to come and get me. You can't imagine how difficult it was. I could have walked away physically at any time, but mentally it's so difficult. They tell you you'll never have a fulfilled life if you leave, and you believe them. It took me a long time to feel anything like normal. I felt guilt, shame and fear."

19 Magazine

2 Put the events of Jane's story in the correct order.

a Jane did a three-week course with the Moonies in Kent. ☐
b Jane left the Moonies. ☐
c Jane rang a friend to ask for help. ☐
d Jane started to spend time with them at the weekends. ☐
e Jane started working full time for the Moonies. ☐
f Jane and her friends went to a Moonies meeting for fun. ☐
g Jane turned eighteen. ☐
h Jane's parents told her to stop seeing the Moonies. ☐
i The Moonies invited Jane to become a member of their organisation. ☐

hanging out spending time
workshop course
euphoric unreasonably happy and excited
brainwashing forcing someone to reject old beliefs and accept new ones
fundraising getting money for the organisation
recruits members
fulfilled enjoyable and satisfying

Key Language Read this sentence from the article.

> ... someone suggested going to a Moonies meeting...

Here *suggest* is followed by a **gerund**. The negative is *suggest not* + gerund.
Example:
Dave suggested not going to the meeting.

We can also use *suggest* (*that*) **+** noun/pronoun **+** *should*(*n't*).

Examples: *Someone suggested we should go to a meeting.*
Dave suggested we shouldn't go to the meeting.

3 Imagine Jane's parents asked you for advice about persuading her to leave the Moonies. Use the prompts to talk about your suggestions.

a don't telephone her; just write to her
I suggested not telephoning her.
I suggested they should just write to her.

b invite her home for the weekend

c don't criticise the Moonies
d don't give her any money
e find out more about the cult
f go to one of the meetings

Talk about it

4 Why do you think the Moonies waited until Jane was 18 before inviting her to join them? Why do you think Jane became a member and why did her parents object? Use evidence from the article, the box below and your own ideas.

THE MOONIES

- The organisation, also known as the Unification Church, has 2-3 million members worldwide and about 500 in Britain.
- Its leader Sun Myung Moon was born in Korea in 1920.
- The first Moonie centres were set up in Britain and the USA in the 1960s.
- Moonies must not drink alcohol, smoke or have sex before marriage.
- Moon, who calls himself The Lord of the Family, claims Jesus appeared to him in a vision and asked him to continue his work on earth.
- Moon says in his book *The Divine Principle* that Jesus died before he could get married and therefore failed to have a perfect family. He claims that he and his wife, known in the group as The True Parents, are putting this right.

5 What is the difference between being in a group like the Moonies and being a member of an established religious group like the Roman Catholic Church? Discuss these points:

- How new and how big is the group?
- Who chooses the leader?
- Is it easy to get clear information about the group?
- Can non-believers participate?
- Do members have to work for it full time?
- Are members brainwashed? Is it easy to leave?

6 Roleplay a conversation between Jane and a friend who is trying to get her to leave the Moonies.

BELIEFS

Tune in

1 Before you listen, name four major religions. Are you a member of one of these faiths? Or are you an atheist or agnostic?

2 Now listen to these three speakers. Write **T** (true), **F** (false) or **?** (don't know) next to each statement.

Alicia

George

Pippa

a believes in Darwin's theory of evolution ☐

b wants to be a scientist ☐

c believes in God ☐

d goes to church once a week ☐

e prays ☐

f believes in an afterlife ☐

g believes in God ☐

h believes in an afterlife ☐

i thinks religion is necessary for a moral sense ☐

j doesn't believe in marriage ☐

k agrees with the Catholic church on contraception ☐

l is not interested in organised religion ☐

m believes in God ☐

n meditates and does yoga ☐

o believes in reincarnation ☐

p isn't superstitious ☐

q believes in astrology ☐

Key Language

Read these sentences from the tape.

> "I don't believe in Adam and Eve... . But I **do** believe in God."
> "My faith **does** help me."
> "I **do** think it's possible... "
> "I **do** believe in reincarnation."

You can use **do/does** and **did** to add emphasis, particularly when you think the listener disagrees or if s/he is doubtful.

Example:
*Really, I **did** enjoy the meeting.*

You can also use **do/does/did** for contrast.

Example:
*I don't believe in heaven and hell, but I **do** believe in reincarnation.*

3 Write five questions about beliefs. You can get ideas from Exercise 2 above.

Example:
Do you believe in an afterlife? Do you go to church regularly?

4 In pairs, ask and answer the questions you wrote for Exercise 3. Where possible, use *do/did/does* in your answers for emphasis or contrast.

5 Do you think it is possible to have strong moral values without having a religion to guide you? Think about your own attitudes to:

- killing
- stealing
- helping people who are weaker than yourself

Are your attitudes based on religious beliefs, your family or school's moral views, the law in your country?

6 In Britain, Christianity is the state religion. By law, every school in England should have a religious service every day and teach religious education. Do you think this is right? What sort of religious education is best in a multi-cultural society?

7 Give a short speech on your beliefs or religious practices.

8 The photos above show four British superstitions. Explain what they are, saying which things are lucky or unlucky. Do you have the same superstitions in your country? Are you or any of your friends and family superstitious? In what way? Why do you think some people are superstitious?

9 Write a questionnaire about beliefs and religious practices. Prepare about 12 questions. Here are some possibilities.

Do you believe in...

God? ☐
an afterlife? ☐

Do you...

pray? ☐
attend religious services regularly? ☐
attend religious services only on special occasions? ☐
If so, which ones? ____

Focus

1 Should we be hard or soft on young criminals? Should we throw them into prison, or should we try to understand and help them?

Read about it

Teenage killers free after 5 months

by Cherry Norton

THE PARENTS of 12-year-old Louise Allen, who was killed last year, have reacted with horror to the news that her killers are to be released on the anniversary of her death.

Louise was kicked to death by two girls in a fairground in Corby, Northamptonshire.

She had intervened to separate two girls who were fighting. A fourth girl joined in, thinking the fight had become a two-against-one affair.

Louise was attacked and kicked repeatedly, once while lying motionless on the ground. She died the next day.

The teenagers were convicted of manslaughter in December, and given a two-year custodial sentence.

The original charge of murder was dropped after extensive negotiations involving the police, defence lawyers and Louise's parents.

The girls will be released on April 30, just five months after being convicted – the term is based on a 12-month reduction for good behaviour and seven months spent in custody before the trial.

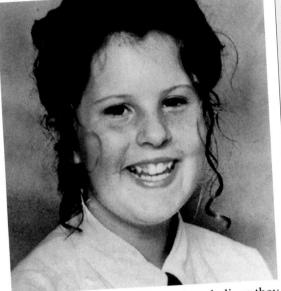

Louise's mother said she could not believe they were going to be released on the first anniversary of Louise's death.

She will visit her grave on Wednesday with her ex-husband John and Louise's brothers, John, 12, and Dean, 2. The family intends to put flowers in the red and white of Manchester United, her favourite football team, on the grave.

THE SUNDAY TIMES

2 Which of these headlines would be suitable for the article? Explain your choice.

a **Shock at 12-year-old girl's death**

b **Anger at early release of killers**

c **LOUISE: MURDER CHARGE DROPPED**

3 Correct these sentences.

a Five girls were involved in the fight.

b The girls were found guilty of murder.

c When they were arrested, they were charged with manslaughter.

d Because of good behaviour, their sentence was reduced by a year and a half.

e They will be released just two years after the crime.

f The family will put flowers at the place where Louise died.

> **anniversary** the same date, one year/two years etc. later
>
> **fairground** park with amusements (eg. the big wheel, ghost train)
>
> **intervened** got involved
>
> **motionless** not moving

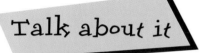

Key Language

Here is some important language for talking about **crime** and **the courts**.

If the police *arrest* you, they *charge* you with a crime; the *charge* could be theft, possession of drugs, murder etc.. In court there are two *lawyers*: one against you, and one representing you – the *defence* lawyer. If the court decides you are not *guilty*, it *releases* you – you are free to go. If the court finds you guilty, it convicts you of the crime. The judge then decides on the *sentence* – eg. how much you must pay (as a *fine)*, or how long you must stay in **prison**. *In custody* (a *custodial* sentence) means in prison or, if you are too young for prison, in a special children's home. *Manslaughter* means killing a person, but it is not as serious as murder – perhaps you wanted to hurt, but not kill, him/her.

4 Use the words in *italics* from the text above to fill the gaps.

a I don't like it in prison. I hope I will be ___ soon.

b They arrested her on a ___ of theft.

c The charge of murder was reduced to ___ .

d A £250 fine wasn't a hard enough ___ .

e You are a danger to the public. I'm giving you a ___ sentence.

f You'll be OK. Get a good ___ lawyer.

Talk about it

5 The two girls who killed Louise were only 11 and 12 years old. Do you think that the sentence was right?

6 Here are some of the sentences possible in an English court.

SENTENCE	What does it mean?
Community service	*You have to do a period (eg. 100 hours) of unpaid work in hospitals/old people's homes*
Fines	*You pay money to the court*
Probation	*You have to stay out of trouble. Once a week you visit a "probation officer", who asks about your behaviour*
Suspended prison sentence	*You don't go to prison immediately, eg. "a six-month sentence suspended for one year" means if you behave well for one year, you are free. If you do something wrong, you go to prison for six months*
Prison	*You go for a fixed period (ranging from a very short period to "life")*

Now look at these cases. If you were a judge, what sentence would you give to these people? Choose from the chart, give full details (eg. a £1000 fine/3 years in prison/one year on probation) and discuss your decision(s).

a 18-year-old Miranda worked in a shoe-shop. She lost her job when she stole £92 from the shop.

b Nigel is 38. He drank a bottle of wine and then drove home. He had a car accident and killed a 13-year-old boy.

c Kevin, 15, was caught travelling on the train without a ticket. The correct ticket would have cost £1.75.

d Stacey, aged 22, was caught selling marijuana at a disco. At her flat about 50 grammes of the drug were found (value: around £250).

e Dean, 17, broke the window of a new Mercedes and stole a mobile phone and four CDs.

f Samira is 32. She killed her husband with a knife while he was asleep. He had been very cruel and violent with her for more than 10 years, and he often had girlfriends.

 **Tune in**

1 Before you listen, think about the death penalty. Does it exist in your country? What sort of crimes are usually considered serious enough for the death penalty?

2 Now listen to Michael Swarovski, a candidate for the Senate in the State of Texas. In this radio interview he gives his views on the death penalty. Is he for or against it?

3 What do these numbers on the tape refer to?

32	500	2	20	100,000	3 million

4 Here are some points on the other side of the argument. What does Mr Swarovski say about each of these points?

a We must not kill a person just to save money.
b A killer can be treated by a psychologist and become a normal person.
c Revenge is not the same as justice. We must look for the right punishment.
d While a prisoner is alive, he has hope.
e The death penalty does not stop killers.

 **Key Language**

Look at this sentence from the tape.

"Would you shoot the clerk?"

You can see that this is a question, but in fact Mr Swarovski is not expecting an answer. This is called a **rhetorical question**. The meaning is
You wouldn't shoot the clerk.

5 Listen to the tape again. Can you hear four more rhetorical questions?

6 Now put these ideas into the form of rhetorical questions.
a We should learn from experience.
b There are enough people in prison already.
c Murderers don't deserve to live in peace.
d We can't forgive people like this.
e This is not the best way to solve the problem.
f You wouldn't actually do the execution yourself.

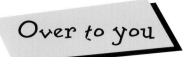
Over to you

7   Britain gave up using the death penalty in 1965. In the argument for and against this issue, what does the table below mean to you?

Murders in England and Wales 1915-1995

Number per million population

Murder (Abolition of the Death Penalty) Act 1965

(y-axis: 4, 6, 8, 10, 12, 14, 16, 18, 20, 22)
(x-axis: 1915, 1925, 1935, 1945, 1955, 1965, 1975, 1985, 1995)

8   The courts sometimes make mistakes, and innocent people are found guilty. Is this an important point in the argument?

9   Some people say the death penalty is against the constitution of the USA, because the constitution forbids "cruel or unusual" punishments. Do you agree that the death penalty is cruel?

10   In different states of the USA, different methods of execution are used, eg. hanging, the electric chair, lethal injection, shooting by firing squad, lethal gas. Which do you find the most and the least acceptable?

11   The last woman to be executed in Britain was Ruth Ellis. She was hanged in 1955. She had shot her lover because he had another girlfriend. It was a "crime of passion". Do you think the death penalty should be used for this type of crime?

Miranda Richardson as Ruth Ellis in the film Dance With A Stranger

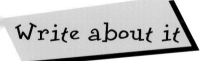
Write about it

12   You are writing a screenplay for a film about a murder. Write the dialogue between a man who is going to be executed tomorrow, and a priest who is visiting him. Start like this:

FATHER PATRICK: How are you feeling, Bruce?

BRUCE: Not too good, Father. I don't want to...

13   Write a letter to Mr Swarovski, either supporting or opposing his views on the death penalty. Start like this:

Dear Mr Swarovski,
I heard your interview on the radio this morning.
I would just like to tell you...

Focus

1 Are there any rules in your house? How strict are your parents compared with your friends' parents?

Read about it

Sex... drugs... alcohol?
What really does go on in a teenager's bedroom?

***Becki Heeley** (16)*
My boyfriend Andy, who's 18, is supposed to be out of my room by 10 pm. We've been going out for six months. We are allowed to be alone in my room but there is a line we don't cross. My mum trusts me, and it would be out of order to take liberties.

Becki's mum, Jane
I don't have many rules about Becki's room, but there are a few. No one's allowed to smoke,

for instance, and friends have to leave by 10pm on school nights and the noise has to be within reasonable levels. She is allowed to have her boyfriend in her room. I don't worry too much about what they do up there because she knows I would kill her. I trust her to behave within reasonable limits.

***Mark Malecki** (19)*
I suppose responsibility is the key word. There aren't rules, as such, but I'm careful about what I leave lying around. They don't like me smoking in the bedroom. I don't smoke much, but I do have cigarettes in there. I have alcohol as well, but most of it was bought as presents by my family. I also keep condoms in the bedroom.

My parents are very fair and I respect that, but drugs are the one thing they wouldn't forgive. I think they are right and I would never bring drugs into the house.

Mark's mum, Maria
Mark frequently has friends round for the evening. He always asks if

he wants to have people over, and he is very good regarding noise. I can't say I am happy about girlfriends staying in his room, but as long as he's discreet and careful, I will put up with it. At his age you have to offer a degree of freedom. Drugs are the only subject where there is no room for discussion – they are absolutely banned, and I trust Mark to be responsible.

Daily Mail

2 Write **T** (true), **F** (false) or **?** (don't know) after each of these statements.

a Becki's boyfriend has to leave her room by 10pm. ☐
b Becki's friends are allowed to smoke in her room. ☐
c Becki's girlfriends can't spend the night at her house. ☐
d Mark's parents prefer him not to smoke in his room. ☐
e Mark is never allowed to have girlfriends staying overnight. ☐
f Mark's parents don't let him play his stereo after midnight. ☐

trusts me	believes that I am honest, sincere
out of order	wrong
take liberties	use one's freedom in the wrong way
behave	say/do things
condoms	contraceptives worn by men
have ... over	invite
as long as	if
put up with	tolerate
a degree of	some

Key Language

There are many different ways of talking about **rules**.
Read these sentences from the article.

Andy ... **is supposed to** be out ... by 10pm...
No one's **is allowed to** smoke.
... friends **have to** leave by 10pm...

They **don't like me** smoking in the bedroom.
Drugs ... **are absolutely banned**...

3 Use verbs from *Key Language* and the prompts **a-o** to talk about rules in your family.
Examples:
I'm allowed to play music after 11pm but it mustn't be too loud.
My sister isn't supposed to go out with her boyfriend during the week.
When I was a teenager, I had to be home from parties by midnight.

a play music
b go out during the week
c be home by
d go out at the weekend
e have parties

f watch TV during the week
g have friends round
h use the telephone
i pay for telephone calls
j have friends stay over

k have boy-/girlfriend stay over
l smoke cigarettes
m help with the housework
n alcohol
o drugs

Talk about it

4 In groups, compare the rules in your families.
Make a list of the five commonest rules. Do you
agree with them? Why/why not?

5 Are there different rules for boys and girls in
the same family? If so, what are the differences
and do you think they are fair?

6 What do/did you argue about with your parents
most often? Describe the worst argument you have
ever had with them.

7 With a partner, make a list of five rules for
parents of teenagers. Tell the rest of the class
why you think each rule is important.

Discipline – Victorian-style!

Tune in

1 Before you listen, think of two school rules about dress and personal appearance. They could be rules at your school/college or one that you know about.

2 Now listen to the news story. Which of these sentences correctly summarises the story?

a A boy was expelled because he wore an earring to school.
b A girl was expelled because she wore a nose ring in an exam.
c A girl was expelled because she wore a nose ring to school.

3 Listen again and put these events in the order they happened by numbering them **1** to **8**. Write **X** for the three events that you do *not* hear about on the tape.

a Sharon got her nose pierced. ☐
b Sharon had to go home. ☐
c Sharon missed her exams. ☐
d Sharon moved to a new secondary school. ☐
e Sharon refused to remove her nose ring. ☐
f Sharon wore her nose ring to school. ☐
g Sharon's brother went to school wearing an earring. ☐
h Sharon's cousin got her nose pierced. ☐
i The headteacher saw Sharon wearing a nose ring. ☐
j The headteacher told Sharon to remove it. ☐
k The headteacher wrote to Sharon's parents. ☐

4 Now listen again and complete these sentences.

a The headteacher ordered Sharon ___ her nose ring or go home.
b *Newsround* asked Sharon ___ her side of the story.
c He asked me ___ immediately.
d He then ordered me ___.
e And he told me ___ to school wearing my nose ring.

Key Language

Read the sentences in Exercise 4 above.
We use the infinitive after words like *tell*, *ask* and *order* when we report an **order** or a **command**.

5 What were the speaker's words in the sentences in Exercise 4?

Example:
a *"Remove your nose ring or go home."*

6 Complete these sentences in as many ways as possible.
a Teachers often tell students to ___ .
b Parents sometimes ask their children to ___ .
c When I'm a parent, I will/won't tell my children to ___ .

Over to you

7 What do you think of Sharon's behaviour?
What would you have done in her situation?
Do you think the headteacher was right to expel her?

8 What are the main rules at your school? Are they written in a rule book? Do you agree with them? Why/why not? Which rule do students break most often? What other rules do you think would be useful?

9 Corporal punishment is forbidden in state schools in Britain. These are some of the usual punishments:

• Detention
• Extra school work
• Suspension
• Unpaid jobs at the school
  (eg. cleaning the classroom)
• Not being allowed to take
  part in certain school
  activities (eg. school
  excursions, sport, music)
• Expulsion

Make a list of punishments that people have received at your school. What had they done wrong? Do you think their punishments were reasonable?

"ASSISTED EDUCATION."

10 Choose one of the following statements and make an argument to support it. You don't have to agree with it! Make a few notes first.

"Giving children freedom turns them into responsible adults."

"Society is becoming more violent because parents and schools are not strict enough."

"Strict parents produce rebellious children."

"The main reason parents are strict with their children is because today's society is very dangerous."

Write about it

11 Imagine you are a student representative at your school. Write a letter to the headteacher complaining about one of the rules. Explain why you and the other students would like the rule changed. Start like this:

Dear Mr ___/Mrs___,
I am writing on behalf of all the students in my year/in the school. We are not happy with the school rule which says that ___. The reason we do not approve of this rule is that ___. We think that it would be better if...

DRINK AND DRUGS

Focus

1 Do you drink alcohol? Do you think there is an alcohol problem among young people?

Read about it

When a drink with dad turns kids into drunks

Another morning, another hangover. Sarah Watson does not enjoy the experience. "It's not very nice being drunk," she says. "You get full of yourself and then you get a headache."

But Sarah is not an adult recovering from a heavy night in the pub. She is 12 and one of a growing number of young children who know the taste – and the effects – of alcohol.

Sarah is one of the lucky ones. She says her experience is relatively limited. But by the time they reach 14, most children have tried alcoholic drinks, according to a nationwide survey on young people and drinking.

Seventy-three per cent of 13- to 14-year-old children interviewed said they had had an alcoholic drink. As many as 55% of 10- to 12-year-olds said they had tried alcohol, and 45% of seven to nine-year-olds.

Experimentation with alcohol begins at an early age, typically in the form of a glass of wine shared with parents.

Drinkline, the national helpline for people with drink problems, said the dangers of alcohol were being overlooked because of concerns about drugs.

Sarah Watson said: "Many people act as though cigarettes can do more damage, and they take time to talk about drugs, but never about alcohol. When adults do talk about it, they just say it's really bad, and that's the end of the conversation."

"I could live without alcohol," said Sharon O'Dea, 15. "But if you go to a party, it is better than taking drugs."

More English teenagers drink alcohol than their contemporaries in France and Spain, according to a report last month.

The Observer/CHILDREN'S EXPRESS

2 Are these sentences true (**T**) or false (**F**)?

a Sarah Watson doesn't like drink, but she likes its effects.
b 26% of children aged 14 have never tried alcohol.
c Almost 50% of nine-year-olds have had an alcoholic drink.
d Young children usually get their first drink from their brothers or sisters.
e According to Drinkline, everybody is now talking about alcohol problems.
f Sharon thinks that drugs are worse than alcohol.

drunks people who get drunk often
hangover headache and tiredness a few hours after drinking too much
full of yourself very self-confident
recovering getting better after an illness
heavy "heavy drinking" = drinking a lot
alcohol all alcoholic drinks (eg. beer, wine, vodka)
helpline a telephone number for people with problems
overlooked missed, not noticed
concerns worries, important considerations
contemporaries people of the same age

Key Language

Look at this sentence from the article.

> ... by the time they reach 14, most children have tried alcoholic drinks...

By + time phrase has the idea of *already*. It is used with the **present perfect** for general statements and the **past perfect** for past facts.

Examples:
By the age of 18 most people have left school.
By 1997 Steffi Graf had won more than $20 million.

3   Here are some facts about the life of Claudia, who is a brilliant mathematician. Use these phrases to complete the sentences.

- learn to speak quite well
- become a university professor
- finish school   • start walking
- get a university degree
- learn to read

a   By the age of six months, ___ .
b   By the age of one year, ___ .
c   By the age of three, ___ .
d   By the age of thirteen, ___ .
e   By the age of fifteen, *she had got a university degree.*
f   By the age of twenty-four, ___ .

4   Complete this sentence in three different ways.
By the age of seven, most children have ___ .

Talk about it

5   Look at this chart. Do you have similar age limits in your country? Do you think the British limits are reasonable? Why/why not? Do a smoking/drinking survey of the students in your class.

6   Drinking alcohol is an accepted social practice in most world countries. But in Libya, Saudi Arabia and other Islamic countries, alcohol is illegal. (It was illegal in the USA from 1920 to 1933 – the Prohibition era.) Make a list of positive and negative points about alcohol.

7   You work for an advertising agency, and you have to create a campaign against Drinking and Driving (driving a car after you have drunk alcohol). In groups, prepare a poster – with a picture and a slogan. Compare your work with other groups and vote for the best campaign.

LEGAL AGE LIMITS IN BRITAIN	
5	drink alcohol at home
16	drink soft drinks in pubs
	drink alcohol with food in restaurants
18	buy alcohol
	drink alcohol in pubs
no limit	smoke cigarettes

Will you be responsible this year?

Every year, thousands are killed, crippled and maimed in drink drive accidents by people who felt OK to drive.

Have none for the road.

35

1 Before you listen, think about heroin. It is derived from opium and is in the same family of drugs as morphine. What is the medical use of such drugs? Do you know anything about heroin addiction?

2 Now listen to Mike talking about being a heroin addict, and answer these questions.

a How does Mike take the drug?
b How did he use to take it?
c How long has he been taking it?

3 Why did Mike start taking heroin? The words in brackets will help you.

a (*social*)
b (*attitude to adults*)
c (*school/job*)
d (*feelings about himself*)

4 Why is it hard for Mike to give up?

a (*physical*)
b (*social*)
c (*daily life*)

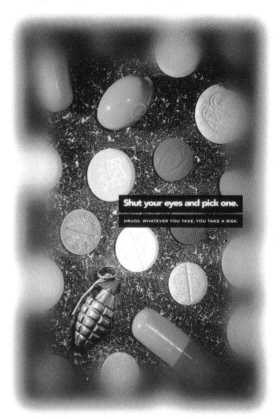

Shut your eyes and pick one.

DRUGS. WHATEVER YOU TAKE, YOU TAKE A RISK.

Look at these sentences from the tape.

> "We'd, you know, dropped out of school... "
> "I mean, that's what they did in the evening... "

In spoken English, people use quite a lot of "fillers" like *you know* and *I mean*. Both these phrases give the speaker time to think. *You know* sometimes shows doubt: it means "Am I using the right word here?"

5 In which of these sentences do the phrases have their original meaning – and in which are they fillers?

a I mean Washington state, not Washington, D.C..
b I mean, they've got, you know, strange ideas.
c Do you know my sister?
d She's, you know, a paramedic or something.
e You know, it's a really good job.
f I mean, the money's not great, but she likes it.

6 Read out this text, adding some fillers. (Note: *I mean* usually goes at the beginning of a sentence. *You know* can go almost anywhere.)

"I started smoking when I was about 13. Lots of kids at school were already smoking by that age. I used to have a puff of my mum's cigarettes. She didn't mind. Then I started buying my own. In the end I was spending all my pocket money on cigarettes."

Over to you

7 The chart below seems to show that cannabis is the biggest problem. But people worry more about ecstasy, cocaine and heroin. Why?

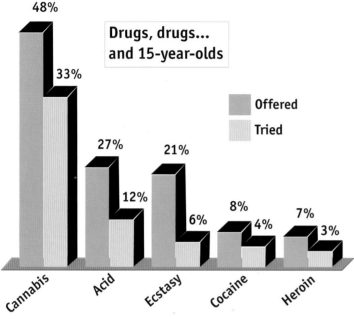

Drugs, drugs...
and 15-year-olds

Offered
Tried

48%
33%
27%
12%
21%
6%
8%
4%
7%
3%

Cannabis   Acid   Ecstasy   Cocaine   Heroin

8 "Addictive" means "very difficult to give up". Do you think nicotine (in cigarettes) is addictive? Why is tobacco legal, when most of the other drugs on the chart are illegal? Would it be a good idea to make tobacco illegal?

9 Some people say that it would be better to legalise all drugs. In that case, you could buy cannabis and other drugs from shops. What would be the advantages and disadvantages of such a change?

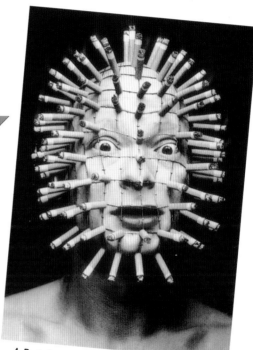
A Dutch anti-smoking campaign poster

Write about it

10 Design an anti-smoking poster for schools or colleges. Sketch a picture or use photos from a magazine; write a slogan and a couple of sentences to go with it.

11 A friend of yours has a problem with alcohol or drugs. Write a letter to the problem page of a magazine, asking for advice. Start like this:

Dear ____,
I'm really worried about my friend Tony (that's not his real name)...

1 What is an "arranged marriage"? In which countries or cultures is this type of marriage common? Do you know anyone who has had an arranged marriage?

Read about it

Real-life COUPLES

Sarita and Ranjit Sharma talk about their arranged marriage

How was the marriage arranged?
Sarita: I was studying in America at the time. A friend of my family told us there was this man living in Britain who was looking for a suitable girl. My dad liked the sound of him. We made some enquiries - his education, what he did, that kind of thing. The news was very encouraging. Ranjit was a good catch.
Ranjit: The first I knew about Sarita was the day before she arrived here! My father organised the whole thing. I was happy to meet Sarita but I knew I could always say no if I didn't think we'd be right together.

What were your first impressions of each other?
Sarita: Good. Although there wasn't a great surge of attraction, I remember thinking, "He seems nice." The atmosphere that day was quite intense because our families were watching us, so Ranjit suggested we go out for a drink on our own.
Ranjit: I liked Sarita. I found her attractive, but there wasn't that spark you get if you see someone you fancy at a party. It was more mental attraction.

How did you decide on each other?
Sarita: We met up three more times over the two weeks before I returned to America - by then I'd decided that Ranjit was right for me.
Ranjit: There was pressure from my family after the very first meeting. I'd seen three girls before Sarita, but she was the first I was interested in. So I said yes after those first three meetings.

Do you love each other now?
Sarita: Yes we do. I couldn't pinpoint an exact time when love began, but it was about two years into the relationship.
Ranjit: Love came into our relationship after a while. I didn't wake up one morning and think, "I love this woman." The love we now have is warm, deep and lasting.

New Woma[n]

2 Read the story again. Write **T** (true), **F** (false) or **?** (don't know) in the boxes next to these statements.

a Sarita and Ranjit had known each other as children.
b Sarita's mother liked Ranjit a lot.
c The first time Sarita and Ranjit met, their families were present.
d They were very physically attracted to each other when they met.
e Sarita and Ranjit agreed to get married after knowing each other for just two weeks.
f They fell in love with each other about two years after their marriage.

---

liked the sound of him liked what he heard about Ranjit
a good catch a good person to marry for reasons of social status
a great surge a sudden, powerful feeling
spark emotional flash
fancy find attractive
pressure strong persuasion
lasting going to continue for a very long time

Key Language

Look at this example of **direct speech**.

"There is this man living in Britain who is looking for a suitable girl."

Now look at this example of **reported speech** from the article.

...A friend told us there was this man living in Britain who was looking for a suitable girl.

3 The table below shows how verb tenses usually change after a reporting verb in the past. Complete the examples.

Direct	Reported
present simple	**past simple**
"He seems nice."	She thought he ___ nice.
"I don't want to get married yet."	He said he ___ want to get married yet.
present continuous	**past continuous**
"My parents are putting pressure on me."	He said his parents ___
present perfect	**past perfect**
"I've met the perfect man."	She said ___
past simple	**past perfect** (*or no change*)
"There wasn't that spark."	He said there ___
can/will	***could/would***
"I can't marry him yet."	She felt that she ___
"I'll have to think about it."	He told his father that he ___

4 Sarita's father is talking to his daughter. Look at his statements. Think of three more, and then change them all into reported speech. Start like this:

Sarita's father told her ___.

a "I have found a suitable young man for you."
b "You will definitely like Ranjit."
c "He lives in England."
d "He has a very good job."
e "He is good looking and quite rich."
f "You can meet him later this month."
g "I have arranged a meeting already."

Talk about it

5 Roleplay the conversation between Sarita and Ranjit when they go out for a drink on their own, the first time they meet.

6 Write a short dialogue between Ranjit and his father after Ranjit's first meeting with Sarita. His father is putting pressure on him to agree to the marriage. Then act the dialogue to the class.

7 Why do you think Sarita and Ranjit's parents like the system of arranged marriages?

8 Imagine your parents are arranging a marriage for you. What questions would you like them to ask about your future husband/wife?

9 Now that you have read the article, what is your opinion of arranged marriages?

Tune in

1 You are going to hear two friends, Jim and Nadia, discussing their parents' divorce. Before you listen, try to guess the reason that Nadia is pleased her parents separated.

2 Now listen to their conversation and answer these questions.
a Who did Jim have a fight with and why?
b Why is Nadia pleased her parents separated?

3 Listen to the tape again and make notes about these questions.

		Jim	Nadia
a	Who do they live with?		
b	When did their parents split up?		
c	What do they think of their parents' new partners?		
d	How do they feel about their mothers?	*wishes he could see mother on her own*	
e	What's their attitude to their parents' divorce?		

4 Use your notes from Question 2 and other information you remember from Jim and Nadia's conversation to describe each family situation. Then take turns to say a sentence each.

Key Language

On the tape, you heard many words connected with family relationships. Here are some of them:

• fall in love   • argue   • break up   • separate   • get divorced

5 Use the words above to make sentences about Jim and Nadia's parents.

6 Fill the gaps in the sentences with words/phrases from the box below.

• half-sisters
• first marriage   • remarried
• single parent
• step-father
• step-mother

a Jim doesn't get on well with his ___.
b Nadia has two little ___.
c Nadia's father has ___ but her mother hasn't.
d Nadia's ___ has three children from her ___.
e Nadia thinks it was hard for her mother being a ___.

Over to you

7 Look at these results from a recent newspaper survey of children's attitudes to divorce. Do a survey of attitudes in your class. Compare your results with the results of the newspaper survey.

Divorce - the side-effects	Children with parents together		Children with parents divorced/separated	
	Agree	Disagree	Agree	Disagree
Marriage should be forever	76%	9%	71%	18%
Children's parents should stay together even if they are unhappy	30%	56%	19%	69%
It is better for children to live with both parents rather than one	77%	10%	59%	22%
It should be made more difficult to get divorced	43%	36%	30%	47%

8 In Britain, people can get married at 16 if their parents agree. They can marry at 18 without their parents' agreement. What age can people marry in your country? Is it right or wrong to get married young? In your opinion, what is the ideal age to get married?

9 Before their wedding, actress Brooke Shields and tennis star Andre Agassi made a contract. They agreed how they will share their £50 million, how much time they will spend in their four houses and how many tennis tournaments Brooke will attend (ten a year).

Do you think it is a good idea to discuss practical details with your future wife/husband before you get married? Why/why not? Make a list of points that you would include in a marriage contract.

Write about it

10 Read this letter to the problem page of a magazine. Write an answer, giving advice.

I am 28 and have been married for seven years. I have two lovely children aged six and four. My problem is that I have fallen out of love with my husband. He does nothing to help in the house, watches TV all the time and drinks too much. He also had an affair with his secretary a few years ago. I nearly left him but I stayed because of the children. I don't want to spend the rest of my days with somebody I don't love but I know my children need both their parents. Please tell me what to do.

Start your answer like this:

"There are two obvious things you can do: stay with your husband, or leave him. If you stay with him... "

1 What do today's fashion models look like? Do you like that look? Why/why not? Are you influenced by fashion?

Read about it

Are today's teenagers victims of fashion?

A survey among the 1,300 pupils at Caldicot Comprehensive School, near Newport, Wales shows that teenage girls and boys are deeply affected by the images presented by the fashion industry in magazines.

When we asked whether super-slim fashion models influence anorexia – the eating disorder in which people go without food – 100 per cent of our sample replied "Yes".

It's not just our schoolmates who hold these views. We interviewed psychologist Dr Glenn Waller of London's Royal Holloway College, an expert on the influence of fashion on adolescents. He told us that fashion photographs in magazines make a huge impact on young people's self-image, particularly females aged 13-19.

"Young people are guided by media standards while they are looking around for an identity," he said. "Magazines provide ideas and these can affect vulnerable people."

"If women look at supermodels who are beanpoles, they may imagine that they themselves are fatter than they really are. If the media used a wider range of female shapes it would be better."

Fortunately, many Caldicot students are not victims of the image-makers. Here's what some of them said:

"If you're constantly dieting, you can't enjoy life."

"Fashion is something kids can control. It is a path many teenagers take to break free and have fun."

"I find nothing attractive about six-foot models who are two stone underweight; they just look ill."

"Friends shouldn't write you off for wearing unfashionable clothes; if they do, they aren't very good friends."

The Daily Telegraph/Caldicot Censored

---

affected influenced
go without food don't eat
sample the people who were interviewed
our schoolmates other pupils at our school
make a huge impact have a big effect

self-image the opinion people have of their own looks
are guided by follow
media standards what they see in magazines/newspapers and on TV
looking around for an identity trying to decide what sort of style to have

vulnerable sensitive
beanpoles very thin
range variety
path road
six-foot 1 metre 83
two stone about 13 kilos
write you off decide you are a failure

---

2 Tick (✓) the six opinions which are expressed in the article. Find the sentences in the story where they are expressed.

a True friends don't expect you to be fashionable. ☐

b You can't blame the fashion business for anorexia. ☐

c Clothes look better on thinner people. ☐

d Dieting takes the fun out of life. ☐

e Fashion allows teenagers to feel free and have fun. ☐

f Fashion models today are getting larger. ☐

g Images of very thin models may make ordinary women feel fat. ☐

h Underweight models are unattractive. ☐

i Pop groups influence teenagers' ideas about fashion. ☐

j The media should show different sizes and shapes. ☐

Key Language

Read this sentence from the article.

They may imagine that they themselves are fatter than they really are.

Comparative words like **fatter** and **more fashionable** can go with a clause (*than*...).

3   Make similar sentences from the prompts.

Example:
There is a big choice of styles now. There didn't use to be a big choice.
There is a bigger choice of styles now than there used to be.

a   She thinks her figure is bad. It isn't bad.
b   He thinks being fashionable is very important. It isn't really very important.
c   She used to be relaxed about her appearance. She isn't so relaxed now.
d   Nowadays young models look unhealthy. They didn't use to look unhealthy.
e   Fashion models are very thin. They shouldn't be so thin.
f   Fashion should be practical. It isn't practical in the fashion magazines.

Talk about it

4   Write **A** (agree) or **D** (disagree) next to each of the statements in Question 2 opposite.
In groups discuss your opinions.

5   Do you follow fashion? Why/why not?

6   Describe someone who you think is a victim of fashion. These ideas may help:

> cost?   comfort?   competitive?
> do the clothes suit the person?
> are they practical?
> is s/he obsessed with fashion?

7   Describe a fashion which you think expresses freedom and fun.

8   Why do you think young people are so interested in fashion?

FASHION

Tune in

1 Before you listen, describe a dress style that you like. It could be your own style or a friend's style.
These words may be useful:

CLOTHES	army trousers Doc Marten boots high heels hipsters platform shoes tops trainers flares

DESCRIBING STYLES	aggressive comfortable ethnic fashionable outrageous practical simple unusual

FABRICS	checked cotton denim flowery leather linen tie-dye

2 Now listen to four people talking about their dress style. Make notes as you listen.
Example:

Maria
Dresses in different style every day. Today ethnic look. Tomorrow maybe army trousers.

3 Listen again to check your notes. Then match the speakers to the photos.

a   b   c   d

4 Listen again and complete these phrases.
a *"Today I've got an ethnic look and I feel very ___ ."*
b *"I may sound like ___ but for me clothes are a status symbol."*
c *"I want to look ___ and I don't mind spending a lot."*
d *"I don't care about looking ___ from other people."*

Key Language

5 Read the sentences in Exercise 4 above and complete this rule.

> After *look, sound*, ___ , we can use an adjective or ___ + a noun.

6 Complete the questions and ask and answer them with a partner.
a What sort of clothes do you feel ___ in?
b Do you care about looking ___ ?
c Do you want to look ___ ?
d Are you more interested in feeling ___ or in looking ___?
e What sort of clothes do you look ___ in?

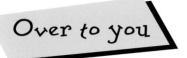
Over to you

7 Give a fashion commentary on one of the outfits shown in this unit.

Example:
"___ *looks very feminine in her Indian skirt. It's very comfortable and the colours go well with her tie-dyed top.*"

8 Choose one of the following statements and make a one minute speech supporting it. You don't have to agree with it! Make a few notes first.

a *"You can know a person's character from their clothes."*

b *"Clothes are becoming more and more aggressive in style."*

c *"Fashion has been greatly influenced by sportswear."*

d *"Young people look as though they are wearing a uniform, they are all so similarly dressed."*

9 Which of these factors are most important when you choose your clothes?
Number them from **1** (most important) to **10** (least important).
Do a survey to find out the top three factors in the class.

comfort ☐
what your friends are wearing ☐
colour ☐
cost ☐
what's available in the shops ☐
material ☐
originality ☐
if the clothes suit you ☐
what pop/TV stars are wearing ☐
fashion magazines ☐

Damon Albern, lead singer with Blur

Iceland's pop star Björk

Write about it

10 Describe the most outrageous thing you've ever worn. What was the occasion and how did people react?

11 Describe your favourite item of clothing. Explain why you like it so much.

Focus

1 Is television good or bad for young children? What effect does it have on them? Did you watch a lot of television when you were small? How much do you let / are you going to let your children watch?

Television exposure damages child speech

by Sarah Boseley

Dr Sally Ward, the country's leading authority on the speech development of young children, believes that babies under one year old should not watch television or videos at all. Children of two or three should watch for no more than an hour a day.

Dr Ward's ten-year study of babies and toddlers in inner-city Manchester showed television was delaying speech development in children. The background noise from televisions stopped them learning to talk as early as they should. At eight months, they neither recognised their names nor basic words like "juice" and "bricks". At three, they had the language of two-year-olds.

Now she has found that children from well-to-do families are being handicapped in the same way. "The television is being used as a babysitter, with nannies particularly. Some of these middle-class children are spending far too much time watching television and videos.

"They get very fixed on the colours and flashing lights. We found in our study it was quite difficult to get them interested in toys."

Parents or minders had stopped talking to them. They were not being taught a basic vocabulary through one-to-one conversations with adults.

All the evidence showed, said Dr Ward, that children whose language was below standard at the age of three could be set back for life.

*The **Guardia***

2 Find the answers in the text to these questions.

a Which of these things are bad for young children?
- juice
- videos
- toys
- television
- inner-city areas
- families

b Which of these are good for young children?
- television
- authority
- background noise
- conversation with adults
- toys

c What language ability does the writer expect a child of eight months to have?

> **toddlers** children aged one to three years old
> **inner-city** the poor parts of the city
> **well-to-do** rich
> **handicapped** damaged
> **nannies** women who look after other people's children
> **minders** nannies or babysitters
> **set back** damaged; slowed down in development

Key Language

Look at this sentence from the article.

> ... children from well-to-do families ... are being handicapped...

The verb phrase *are being handicapped* is the **passive continuous** form.
Can you find two other sentences in the article which contain the passive continuous?

3 Use these verbs to fill the gaps with passive continuous forms.

- force
- give
- neglect
- watch
- leave
- criticise
- teach

Example:
Television channels are being criticised for not making more educational programmes.

a Parents are busy, so children ___.
b Toddlers (not) ___ enough quiet time with their parents.
c Parents ___ to spend more time at work.
d Many kids ___ alone to watch television.
e Much of the time, the TV (not really) ___.
f Some children (not) ___ how to play.

4 Using the passive continuous, make sentences about these subjects:

- footballers
- my brother/sister
- many politicians
- some students
- old people
- I
- women

Examples:
Footballers are being paid too much these days.
My sister is being asked to pay for her university studies.

Talk about it

5 Two-year-old children don't have very much to say. Why do you think it is important for them to speak?

6 Does the article reflect your own experience of young children and television?

7 Is it possible that Dr Ward's research is wrong? Can you think of any problems with this kind of research (eg. the evidence, or the attitudes of the researchers)?

"Well, you did say they should go outside and get some fresh air"

8 Critics of television are not only worried about young children. How would you answer these comments? Prepare some notes and then discuss the issue in class.

"Watching TV is completely passive. You don't have to do anything."
"We're all becoming couch potatoes."
"Teenagers should be creating their own entertainment."

🔊 Tune in

1 Before you listen, think about some films or TV programmes you have seen recently. Which ones contained scenes of violence? Was the violence necessary?

2 Now listen to Lucinda McIntosh, who is the secretary of an organisation called PAVIM, "Parents Against Violence in the Media". <u>Underline</u> the words she uses from this box:

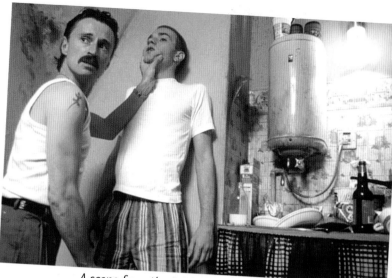

A scene from the British film Trainspotting

death	dead	guns	violent	terrible	blood	knives	sadistic	crimes
disgusting	shot	killers	murders	violence	brutal	copycat		

3 Here are some comments by George Winter, a director who has made a series of gangster films containing a lot of violence. He disagrees totally with Lucinda McIntosh. Listen to the tape again and write down the points which answer these comments.

a "If anything, society used to be more violent than it is now. People used to go and watch public executions."

b "You just can't blame one particular movie for one particular crime. There are so many influences in each case."

c "Kids are very clever about the media. They know very well what is real and what is not real."

d "You see a marriage in a movie. Does that make you go straight out and get married? I don't think so! It's not that simple."

e "There is simply no real evidence for a connection between television violence and real life crimes."

Key Language

Look at these sentences from the tape.

> "Films have a powerful effect on all of us."
> "They make you laugh."
> "Why shouldn't they make you violent?"
> "Films can cause you to change your life-style."

Here are some more ways of talking about the results of experience.

"The newspaper article gave me the idea of working abroad."

"That book influenced me. In fact my parents were influenced by it, too. It was an important influence on all of us."

4 Complete these sentences using your own ideas.

a When I broke my arm, the pain made me ___ .

b The people who have influenced me most are ___ .

c A television documentary gave me the idea of ___ .

d Problems at home caused my sister to ___ .

e The type of films which have a powerful effect on me are ___ .

f Television is a bigger influence on young people than ___ .

Over to you

5 Why is there so much violence in films and on television? Why do viewers like it?

6 Look at this chart, showing the opinions of New Yorkers between the ages of 16 and 45. Does it surprise you?

7 Carry out a quick survey in your class, asking the same question. How similar are your results to the chart?

8 How much do you agree with the views of Lucinda McIntosh? Does TV violence cause real violence?

Do you think there is too much violence on TV?

Females
Yes 84%
No 12%
Don't know 14%

Males
Yes 61%
No 23%
Don't know 16%

9 Look at this cartoon. Do you think it is realistic? Why/why not? It's a joke, but what is the serious point behind it?

All this violence on TV is a bad influence on you.

Move away from the TV set. Put your hands in the air.

10 What should be done about screen violence? Should it be censored? Is there a difference between TV programmes, video and films at the cinema?

Write about it

11 Describe a violent scene from a programme or a film which you have seen recently.

12 *"By watching violence, you get it out of your system. Violent films make you calmer and less violent in your own life."*

Write a paragraph either for or against this point of view.

13 A lot of people have complained to TV companies about violent images in news broadcasts. Some television companies have now stopped using pictures in war and crime reports. Write a letter to a TV company to support or oppose this change. You could start like this:

Dear Sir or Madam,
I think it is ridiculous that we are not allowed to see informative pictures from war zones...

Focus

1 How many people in the class are vegetarians? When did they become vegetarian? Do you think the number of vegetarians is increasing?

Read about it

Children of the Corn

A survey done this summer by Teenage Research Unlimited found that 35 percent of girls and 18 percent of boys thought being veggie was "in". Concern for animals is the leading reason kids give up eating meat.

In the last decade, animal-rights groups have made teenagers a prime target. At big rock concerts, People for the Ethical Treatment of Animals (PETA) shows stomach-turning footage of the worst slaughterhouses. Amy Kennedy, 20, of Philadelphia, vividly recalls seeing its videos three years ago. "I knew instantly that I would never eat meat again." Most veggies are indignant about factory-farming practices like debeaking chickens and clipping the tails off pigs.

Usually, moms and dads aren't too thrilled about their kids' vegetarianism. "It scares them," says Dr David Herzog of Massachusetts General Hospital. But getting enough protein – usually parents' biggest fear –

is not a problem. It is plentiful in the whole grains vegetarians are so fond of. Iron and zinc are a more serious consideration, however, since they are most concentrated in animal flesh.

Most adolescent veggies have the same problems as their carnivorous peers: they like junk food. High school vegetarians, who complain about the limited options in their cafeterias, report that greasy cheese pizza and peanut-butter sandwiches (both high in fat as well as protein) are their staples.

Giving up meat can sometimes be a warning sign of something more serious, like an eating disorder. Experts say many young women who suffer from anorexia start out as vegetarians.

Fortunately, most teen vegetarians face more mundane problems – like fitting into the family's eating routine. In the Ahkami household in southern California, mom Linda prepares two dinners most nights – one for her two vegetarian daughters, and another with meat for her husband. "It can be a nuisance," she admits.

Newsweek

---

veggie abbreviation for "vegetarian"
in fashionable
animal-rights groups people who want animals to get better treatment
made ... a prime target tried to influence
stomach-turning footage films that make you feel sick
slaughterhouses buildings where animals are killed for meat
factory-farming farms where animals are kept in small cages
practices methods
debeaking cutting off the beaks
clipping cutting

thrilled happy
peers people the same age
junk food bad quality, unhealthy food
greasy covered in oil
peanut-butter cream made from peanuts (usually eaten on bread)
their staples the food they eat most often
anorexia psychological illness that makes people refuse to eat (commonest among teenage girls)
mundane ordinary

2 Correct each of these statements.

a Most teenagers stop eating meat because they are worried about their health.

b At rock concerts, some animal-rights groups show videos of terrible diseases you can get from eating meat.

c Most parents are worried that their children will not get enough vitamins if they are vegetarians.

d Teenagers say there is a big selection of high quality vegetarian food in their school cafeteria.

e Giving up meat is always a sign of a psychological problem.

f Linda Ahkami cooks vegetarian food for the whole family every night.

Key Language

Read these sentences from the article. You will see that the relative pronoun ***that*** is left out.

> Concern for animals is the leading reason (that) kids give up eating meat.
> It is plentiful in the whole grains (that) vegetarians are so fond of.

3 Complete these sentences where the relative pronoun *that* can be left out.

a The reason (*that*) I eat a lot of ___ is that ___ .

b The kind of food (*that*) I like best is ___ .

c The first time (*that*) I ate ___, I ___ .

d One reason (*that*) people become vegetarians is that ___ .

e One thing (*that*) I can't eat is ___ .

f The most unusual food (*that*) I've ever eaten was ___ .

g The thing (*that*) I don't like about (vegetarians/ eating meat/modern farms/school food) is that ___ .

Talk about it

4 Do you think it is wrong to kill animals for food? Why/why not? Is it more acceptable to eat fish and some types of meat than others? Is it wrong to kill animals for leather?

5 Do you agree with the vegetarians who avoid eating meat for health reasons? Why/why not?

6 Read about these two practices on factory farms? What do you think about them? Do you think they're a good way of keeping the price of meat down? Are they a good reason to give up eating meat?

Pigs are locked in metal cages and made to reproduce every eight weeks. They are kept indoors and cannot turn around. The piglets are taken away from them at three weeks.

20,000 chickens are kept in one shed. They are bred and fed so that they are ready for the slaughterhouse at seven weeks. For the last week of their life they do not move much because they are so heavy.

FOOD

 Tune in

1 Before you listen, describe a typical lunch at your school, college or office canteen.

2 Now listen to this radio report about children's eating habits and look at the pictures. Which things are mentioned?

3 Read through the list of arguments below. Now listen again and tick (✓) the arguments you hear. Write **X** for any arguments that you do *not* hear.

a Too many children eat hamburgers and chips. ☐
b Overweight children may get heart problems later. ☐
c Sugar is bad for the teeth. ☐
d In self service canteens, school children copy what their friends eat. ☐
e Sugary food doesn't contain as much fibre as fruit and vegetables. ☐
f TV advertisements have a bad influence on children's diets. ☐
g Some additives make children too active. ☐
h Some parents are teaching their children bad eating habits. ☐

Key Language

4 Listen to the tape again, if necessary, and complete these sentences with **too much**, **too many**, **enough** or **more**.

a British schoolchildren eat ____ sugar and animal fat.
b They also consume ____ additives and colourants.
c Eating ____ fat can make you overweight.
d Children who eat ____ sweets don't get ____ fibre.
e ____ schools should sell fruit in their shops.
f Schools should spend ____ time on food education.
g ____ children eat crisps and biscuits for their evening meal.
h Some parents should take ____ trouble over their children's food.

5 Use language from Exercise 4 to talk about food in your family, school or country. Ask and answer questions.

Examples:
I think people eat too much meat in this country.
I think the canteen should serve more salads.

52

Over to you

6   The British eat more fast food than any other Europeans, spending on average £2.5 billion each year on burgers, takeaway chicken, fish and chips and pizza. The French come second and the Germans third. How much do you think you spend a year on fast food? What is your favourite fast food? Do you think it is healthy?

7   Roleplay a conversation between somebody who wants to go out to eat fast food and somebody who wants to buy food and prepare it at home.

8   Choose one of the following statements and prepare an argument to support it. (Don't worry if you don't believe in it!) Make a few notes first.

"American food like burgers and cola is taking over the world. It's time we remembered our own national dishes."

"Cooking and eating is a waste of time. Life will be perfect when we can swallow a few pills instead of eating food."

"TV advertisements for crisps, chocolate bars and fizzy drinks should be banned."

9   What does this cartoon mean? Do you find it funny?

"Ere, take this back, it's got a flavour of something."

Write about it

10   Write a newspaper or radio advertisement for a new restaurant. Give the restaurant a name and describe some of its specialities. Start like this:

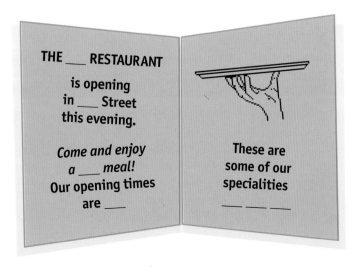

THE ___ RESTAURANT
is opening
in ___ Street
this evening.

Come and enjoy
a ___ meal!
Our opening times
are ___

These are
some of our
specialities

___ ___ ___

1 How do you get on with new people? What if you have to live or work together? Do you become friends – or drive each other mad?

Read about it

Living with a stranger

Thrown together, roommates can become the best of friends – or enemies

The roommate situation is the first challenge students face. Learning to tolerate a stranger's idiosyncrasies may teach flexibility and the art of compromise. But the learning process is often painful. At Ithaca College in Upstate New York, Julie Noel and her roommate were uncommunicative and uncomfortable throughout the year. "I kept my stereo up once for a whole day just to test her because she was so timid," says Noel. "It took her until dinnertime to finally turn it off." Near year's end, the two ended up in a screaming fight. "Looking back, I wish I had talked to her more about how I was feeling," says Noel.

Most roommate conflicts spring from such small, irritating differences. Suzie Orr, director of housing at Indiana's St Mary's College, says that the matching process is complicated: "Do you put together people who are similar – or different, so they can learn about each other?"

Alan Sussman at the University of Maryland says: "I think they must have known each of our personalities and picked the opposite." While Sussman was neat and a compulsive studier, his roommate was messy and liked to party into the early hours. Sussman considered moving out at the end of the semester, but decided to stay and "fight it out". Against all odds, the two ended up being friends. Says Sussman: "We taught each other a lot."

There are many stories of college roommates becoming lifelong friends. Singers Jean Norris and Renee Neufville of the soul duo Zhane started writing songs while rooming together at Temple University in Philadelphia. After breaking up with their boyfriends within 24 hours of each other, they managed to compose their way out of the blues.

U.S.News & World Report

2 Match the people with the facts.

a Suzie Orr   didn't like her shy roommate

b Jean Norris   tries to put the right students together

c Julie Noel   is very tidy, unlike his roommate

d Alan Sussman   ended up working with her roommate

---

idiosyncrasies somebody's individual qualities/habits (eg. sleeping with the window open)
flexibility being happy to change; easy with other people
compromise half way between two points of view
conflict disagreement, fight
spring from come from/originate from
matching putting two suitable compatible people together
compulsive doing something all the time; unable to stop
semester (AmE) term (part of the college year)
against all odds although it was very improbable
compose their way out of the blues avoid sadness by writing songs

3 This article contains three mini-stories. Decide which of them have happy endings, and which has a sad ending.

a Julie Noel and her Roommate
b Alan Sussman and his Roommate
c Jean Norris and Renee Neufville

Now retell one of those mini-stories to the rest of the class – *without* looking back at the article!

Key Language

Look at this sentence from the article.

> ... I wish I had talked to her more about how I was feeling...

I wish + **the past perfect** is a good way of talking about regrets. Bad things happened, or you made mistakes, and sadly it is too late to change things now.

4 Re-phrase these sentences starting with *I wish*... .

a She never told me when she was upset.
  I wish she had told me when she was upset.
b I didn't ask her about her problems.
c Her other friends didn't want me in their group.
d They said horrible things about me.
e I forgot her birthday.
f I wasn't strong enough to keep our friendship going.

5 Do you have any regrets? Of course you do! Talk about one thing in your life you wish you *hadn't* done, and one thing you wish you *had*.

Talk about it

6 What "idiosyncrasies" do you find irritating in other people? Which of these people would really annoy you?

* *"He plays nothing but rap music."*
* *"She loves to complain and criticise – she's always negative."*
* *"She doesn't really listen when you speak to her."*
* *"He stops in front of every mirror and looks at himself."*
* *"He can't accept any sort of criticism. He is always right."*
* *"She leaves her clothes everywhere around the house."*
* *"She never wants to eat the same thing as everyone else."*

7 Make your own list of the most irritating things about people in your life – friends, family, or just people you know. Then say what you like about the same people.

8 Mahatma Gandhi said *"The only really lasting and valuable friendship is between people of a similar nature."* In the article, Susie Orr is not so sure of this. What do you think?

9 The English poet William Blake (1757-1827) wrote:
I was angry with my friend.
I told my wrath, my wrath did end.
I was angry with my foe.
I told it not; my wrath did grow.

Can you explain the meaning of the poem? (*wrath* = anger, *foe* = enemy) Do you agree with the idea?

Tune in

1 Before you listen, think about friendship between women. Is it different from friendship between men?

2 Now listen to Laura and James being interviewed.
Who has these opinions?
Write **L** for Laura, **J** for James, or **B** for both.

a Talking about your problems is a sign of weakness. ☐

b Girls and boys have different kinds of friendships. ☐

c Boys' friendships don't last as long. ☐

d It doesn't matter if friendships last a long time. ☐

e It's important to tell your friends your secrets. ☐

Girls' friendships: are they special?

3 What are the two main points that Laura makes about the differences between boys and girls?

Key Language

Look at this sentence from the tape.

"It would make me seem weak and pathetic, telling my friends."

The gerund (the **-ing** form) is at the end of the sentence. This often happens in speech.
But in writing, we usually put the gerund at the beginning, like this:
Telling my friends would make me seem weak and pathetic.

4 Listen to the tape again. Can you hear two more examples of the same structure?

5 Turn these sentences round, putting the gerund phrase at the end.

a Making new friends can be difficult.
   It can be difficult, making new friends.

b Keeping in touch with your friends is very important.

c Just listening to their problems can often help people.

d Thinking about the fights I have had with friends upsets me.

e Being ready to help is a sign of real friendship.

6 Now make some examples of your own using these phrases.

a It really hurts, ____ .

b It makes me uncomfortable, ____ .

c It must be difficult, ____ .

d It's one of the saddest things, ____ .

e It's not something that boys do well, ____ .

Over to you

7 What do you think of Laura's ideas?
Do a survey of boys and girls in your class.
Are their reactions to what she says different?

8 James says that he "grows out of"
old friends. How does that happen?
Does it happen to you?

9 When a girl gets a boyfriend, does that
often affect her other friendships? And what
about when a boy gets a girlfriend?

10 Which of these quotations or proverbs do you agree with? Say why/why not.

a *"Friendship never ends."* (The Spice Girls)
b *"Money can't buy friendship."*
c *"A faithful friend is the medicine of life."* (Ecclesiasticus)
d *"A friend is a person with whom I may be sincere."* (Ralph Waldo Emerson)
e *"The only way to have a friend is to be one."* (Ralph Waldo Emerson)
f *"Old friends are best."*
g *"Good neighbours become good friends."* (The title song of *Neighbours*, a TV soap opera)

Write about it

11 Read this letter to Sandy, an "agony aunt" working for a magazine.

Dear Sandy,
I don't know what to do. Emma and I have been best friends for years. We do everything together. But now things are going wrong. Two months ago I started going out with a gorgeous boy called Darren. I'm crazy about him. The problem is that Emma really likes him, too. I can't help noticing the way they look at each other. We've always discussed everything in the past, but we don't talk about him – it's almost a forbidden subject. If they get together, I'm going to lose my best friend AND my boyfriend – I can't bear to think about it. Please help me.

Catherine

Ask Sandy!

Imagine you are Sandy.
Write to Catherine, giving her some advice.

12 Write about a friend of yours. What do you like about her/him? And what about negative points?
Try to explain why you get on well together.

1 Do you live in a place with traffic jams? Do you know about any other environmental problems caused by cars?

Read about it

LEAVE YOUR CAR AT HOME!

In the last hundred years, cars have revolutionised the way we travel... but at what cost? If you're a driver, using your car less is one of the most important things you can do to help the environment – and help make it easier for everyone to get around. Here's why.

IT'S A CHOKE!

Car fumes are the leading cause of smogs, which are choking our towns and cities, and a major contributor to poor air quality in rural areas, threatening the health of one in five people.

Pregnant women, young children and people who suffer from heart and lung disease are most at risk.

GOING NOWHERE

With 21 million cars already clogging up UK roads, travelling can be a slow and frustrating experience. If we don't do anything to cut car use, there could be more than 30 million cars competing for road space by the year 2025.

Road congestion already costs our economy some £15 billion every year.

CLIMATE CATASTROPHE?

Road traffic is the fastest growing cause of carbon dioxide, the main "greenhouse gas". Rising levels of greenhouse gases in our atmosphere threaten to make the Earth hotter, leading to disastrous changes in the world's climate.

Cars pump out 14% of all the UK's carbon dioxide pollution.

CARMAGEDDON

Making cars, producing fuel and building roads gobbles up precious natural resources, destroys and poisons huge areas of land.

In the UK, road building threatens to damage or destroy over 50 of our finest wildlife reserves.

WHAT A WASTE!

When cars are scrapped, many materials end up in the ground or burnt, poisoning our air, water and soil with harmful chemicals.

Each year 1,400,000 cars are scrapped worldwide.

FRIENDS *of the* earth

2 Which five points about cars are made by the article? Put a tick (✓) in the boxes.

a They're ugly. ☐
b They cause pollution. ✓
c There are too many of them. ✓
d They cause health problems. ✓
e They're noisy. ☐
f They're too expensive for ordinary people. ☐
g They're bad for wildlife. ✓
h They contribute to climate change. ✓
i They make people lazy. ✓

choke not being able to breathe
rural in the country (not the city)
threatening risking
clogging up blocking
congestion heavy traffic (= traffic jams)
pollution things which damage the environment
fuel petrol
gobbles eats greedily
resources useful natural things (eg. metals, oil)
scrapped destroyed
soil the earth in which plants grow
harmful dangerous (for people, animals or plants)

3 The article recommends "using your car less". Which harmful effects are reduced if you do that? Make a list from information in the text.

Key Language

Look at this sentence from the article.

> In the last hundred years, cars have revolutionised the way we travel...

To talk about a period of past time which comes up to the present, we use the **present perfect**. This is very useful when discussing modern technology, or changes in the environment.

4 Match up these time phrases and clauses. Choose the best combinations.

a Over the last 300 years...
b Since 1900...
c Since the invention of the telephone, ...
d Since world leaders met at Rio, ...
e Recently...
f In the last two or three years...

1 *d.* they have done very little for the environment.
2 *b* the car has replaced the horse.
3 *f.* the Internet has developed dramatically.
4 *a.* technology has completely changed our lives.
5 *c.* communication has got cheaper and quicker.
6 *e.* I've started cycling to work.

5 Fill the gaps with a time phrase or a clause using the present perfect. Talk about technology, or events in your own life.

a ___ CDs have replaced LPs.
b Since I learnt how to use a computer ___ .
c ___ mobile phones have become very popular.
d In the last ten years ___ .
e ___ I've become very interested in "green" issues.

Talk about it

6 Why do people love cars so much? Is it because they are convenient means of transport – or do they have other qualities? (Think about car adverts.) Do a survey in your class to find out.

7 Is it possible to "use cars less"? In groups, discuss these ideas :
- provide good public transport
- make it difficult for car users (eg. expensive parking)
- cut down the need for journeys (eg. new technology)

8 The article talks about damage to the environment even if we don't use cars much. Discuss one or more possible solutions to this problem.

9 Who should solve these problems – governments or individuals? Would you rather join a political campaign, or do something about it yourself, instead?

59

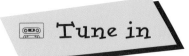

Tune in

1 Before you listen, think about tropical rainforests. Where are they? What are they like? Why are they in the news?

2 Now listen to Rebecca Walker, who has made several TV programmes about the destruction of the rainforests. Which of these sentences are true (**T**) and which are false (**F**)?

a The "canopy" of the forest means the tops of the trees. ☐

b 25% of all animal and plant species live in the rainforest. ☐

c There are more than 4,000 types of tree. ☐

d We get medicines from plants in the rainforest. ☐

e A treatment for AIDS has been discovered in the rainforest. ☐

f We have lost over half the world's rainforests since 1945. ☐

g The forest "breathes in" oxygen, like humans. ☐

3 Look at the six points below. Rebecca mentions three of them. Which ones? Listen again and identify them, and then explain each one.

- beauty for visitors
- danger of climate change
- full of dangerous animals
- good place to get wood
- home of native Amerindian people
- important for medical science

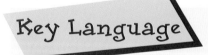

Key Language

Look at this sentence from the tape.

"We must stop now, **or** it will be too late."

There are several forms which mean the same:

"We must stop now; **otherwise** it will be too late."
"We must stop now; **if** not, it will be too late."
"We must stop now; **if** we don't, it will be too late."
"**If** we don't stop now, it will be too late."

4 Can you remember a sentence from the tape which includes the word *otherwise*?

5 Rewrite these sentences cutting out *if* and using *otherwise/or*.

a If we don't change our attitude, there will be an ecological disaster.

b If we don't save these animals, our grandchildren will blame us.

c If we don't use energy more carefully, pollution will continue to increase.

d If we don't respect the Earth, it will die.

e If we don't think about the future, we won't have one.

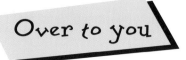

Over to you

6 Farmers in Brazil want to cut down the forest to make room for agriculture. Tourists want to keep the forest so that they can see the wildlife. In groups, prepare the arguments on each side, and then talk about the issue in class.

7 Many people in Britain think that tropical countries should preserve their rainforest. But those countries sometimes say: "You in Britain have cut down all your forest. You have no right to tell us what to do." It is true that 6,000 years ago, Britain was covered in forest, and now only a tiny area remains. How do you feel about this argument?

8 What can *you* do to prevent the destruction of the rainforest? Make a list of ideas, then discuss and decide which are the most useful.

9 Here is a short list of environmental or "green" issues. Which do you think is the most important? Explain your choice to the class.

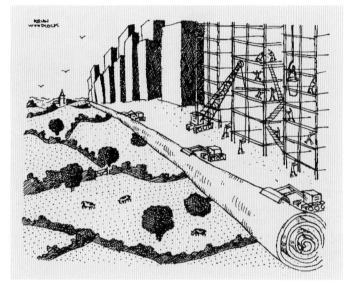

Which point in Question 9 goes with this picture?

- climate change – global warming, or "the greenhouse effect"
- acid rain
- species in danger of extinction (eg. the rhino, the elephant, the tiger)
- destruction of the rainforest
- destruction of the countryside
- pesticides and other pollution in food

10 It is sad when an animal or plant species becomes extinct. But we don't feel bad about the dinosaurs – and *they* disappeared millions of years ago. Does it really matter if we lose a few more species?

Write about it

11 Design a T-shirt with a message about the rainforest or about another green issue.

12 Think of a beautiful natural place that you know. Write a description, including the plants and animals that live there.

1 Have you ever found money or a wallet in the street? What did you decide to do with it?

Read about it

Rich pickings, poor standards?

Honesty, as the Reader's Digest has demonstrated by leaving 80 wallets containing £30 around the country, is both absent and alive in the most surprising places. The poor, like Glasgow student Andrew Pryde who had only £10 to spend on food that week, often found it in themselves to return the wallet, while those who were obviously much better off sometimes trousered the money without a second thought.

Trouser is the right word here because it seems that women are far more likely to be honest than men. (Two thirds of women who found a wallet handed it in compared to little more than half of men.)

Imagination often seemed to separate the people in the Reader's Digest experiment. The Glasgow student wondered if the wallet might have sentimental value, while an unemployed man in Basildon speculated that it might have been dropped by someone else who was unemployed.

What would you do in the following situations?

1 You find a £5 note lying in the street. Do you **a**) hand it into the police? **b**) pocket it and thank your good fortune? **c**) give it to charity or the next homeless person you meet?

2 You have filled in a £5 National Lottery ticket for a friend who has asked you to choose his numbers. At the same time you have completed your own ticket. Three days later you discover that one of the tickets has come up with five numbers, but you can't be absolutely certain whether it is your ticket, or your friend's. A prize of more than £100,000 is involved. Do you **a**) suggest that you split the prize? **b**) make the claim yourself and keep the whole amount? **c**) insist that your friend takes the whole amount?

The **Guardian**

2 Find the answers in the text to these questions.

a What was the Reader's Digest experiment on honesty?
b Who were generally more dishonest - men or women?
c Why did Andrew Pryde hand the wallet in?
d How did the man in Basildon react?

---

rich pickings   money which people get easily but dishonestly
poor standards   bad moral attitudes
found it in themselves   made a moral decision
better off   richer
trousered   kept (literally, "put inside their trouser pockets")
has ... numbers   has the five winning numbers
split   share equally
make the claim   ask for the money

Read this sentence from the article.

> What would you do in the following situations?

We use **would** or **'d** when we imagine a situation or action. Often there is an **if**-clause with the **past simple** in the same sentence.

Examples:
If I found a £5 note in the street, I would hand it in.
I'd buy a boat if I won £100,000 in the lottery.

3 Use the prompts to make questions with *if* + past simple and *would*.

a shop assistant (*give*) you too much change by mistake / what you do?

b you (*see*) someone cheating in an exam / you report them?

c you (*crash*) your motorbike into an expensive car and nobody (*see*) you / you tell the police?

d your rich friend (*forget*) he had lent you £20 / you remind him?

e how you feel / you (*lose*) your wallet containing £50?

f you tell the waiter / he (*forget*) to charge you for your drink?

4 In pairs, ask and answer the questions above. Give reasons.

Talk about it

5 Do you think the Reader's Digest experiment was a good way of checking on people's honesty?

6 Do you agree that women are more honest than men? Why/why not?

7 What would you do in the situations described in the last two paragraphs of the article? Would you choose one of the options or take some other action?

8 Have you, or has anyone you know, ever lost money or something valuable? What happened? Did you/(s)he ever get it back?

9 Do you think it would be excusable for a very poor person to keep a wallet found in the street?

63

1 Before you listen, think of two actions: one that you consider only a little dishonest and one that you consider very dishonest.

2 Now listen to a radio discussion about honesty and tick (✓) the actions that are mentioned. Write **M** (Michael), **S** (Sylvia) or **L** (Louise) next to an action that s/he has done.

a   Cheating in an exam ☐
b   Travelling on a train/bus without a ticket ☐
c   Reading private letters without permission ☐
d   Keeping the change when the assistant gives back too much ☐
e   Drinking alcohol under age ☐
f   Watching an 18-rated film under age ☐
g   Stealing from a shop ☐
h   Lying to parents ☐
i   Copying a friend's homework ☐

On the tape you can hear several ways of expressing moral attitudes. Listen again and complete the speakers' actual words.

I'm scared of getting caught. But I don't think ___

I lied about my age. But I don't think ___

Michael

I totally ___ who don't pay the proper fare.

Sylvia

Louise

3 Use the phrases below and the actions in Exercise 2 (**a-i**) to ask questions about honesty. Then use the speakers' phrases for some of your answers.

Have you ever ___ ?
Would you ever ___ ?
Do you think it's always right/wrong to ___ ?

Example:
Would you ever cheat in an exam?
No, I wouldn't. I totally disapprove of people who do that. They should...

4 Roleplay this situation. You find a £50 note in the street. You decide to keep it. Your friend thinks you should hand it in to the police station.

5 Put these actions in order of dishonesty: **1** for the least dishonest and **6** for the most. Discuss your list.

Stealing £5 from a friend's jacket. ☐
Keeping £5 that you find in the street. ☐
Stealing something worth £5 from a shop. ☐
Keeping quiet when a cashier gives you £5 too much change. ☐
Stealing £5 from your parents. ☐
Not paying back £5 you borrowed from a friend. ☐

6 Do a class survey. Find out which of these actions your classmates have done/would do.

Lying to their parents/partner about where they're going ☐
Lying about their age to get into an 18 film ☐
Not admitting that they have broken/damaged something ☐
Copying from someone in a public exam ☐
Not telling people the truth (to avoid upsetting them) ☐
Reading letters or a diary without permission ☐
Repeating something they've promised to keep secret ☐
Lying about their age to make themselves more attractive ☐

7 A friend of yours regularly shoplifts. You don't approve but you don't know how to stop him/her. Write a letter to the problem page of a magazine. In 50–100 words, explain the situation and ask for advice. Start like this:

> Dear ____ ,
> I have a friend who has a terrible habit: shoplifting. Sometimes s/he goes into ____ shops and takes ____ . She/He also steals ____ from ____ shops...

8 The police have just returned your lost wallet. Write a letter to the person who handed it in, thanking him/her. Explain how worried you were after losing it. Start like this:

> Dear ____ ,
> Thank you so much for handing in my wallet to the police station. When I lost it last Wednesday I was very worried. I thought...

Focus

1 English is becoming a world language. Is this good news for everyone, or can it cause problems?

Read about it

No Getting Around It: English Is Global Tongue

by the Marqués de Tamarón

Most of us feel that our own language is an essential part of our national identity, yet at the same time we realize that we need a world language, a sort of lingua franca.

Over the centuries, Greek, Latin, Spanish, French, Malay, Swahili and other languages have been used as international instruments for trade, diplomacy or religion. Many of them are still used in that capacity.

But three new elements have complicated the situation. The first is the rise of English to the position of world language. This makes life easier for many people, but it irritates others. Many speakers of less widespread languages feel threatened by English. It is like sleeping next to an elephant; regardless of its intentions, the size of the animal makes it dangerous.

Speakers of minority languages quite rightly fear the disappearance of their cultural identity. According to Michael Krauss of the Alaska Native Language Center, nine out of ten of the 6,000 languages in the world will die out within the next century. This is the second new element in the linguistic situation.

The third, more dangerous, novelty is the modern reluctance to accept multilingualism. Why shouldn't a Corsican use Corsican in some cases and French in others? Indeed, why should a Frenchman feel dishonored using English to sell Camembert to a Japanese?

Nowadays, linguistic rivalry is the third most common cause of conflict, after race and religion, and is often mixed with the other two. It need not be so.

Everyone is right in trying to preserve his or her vernacular tongue. But this should not exclude other languages. Speakers of minor languages will also have to learn a major language to profit from the expanding world economy.

INTERNATIONAL **Herald Tribune**

2 Which of these alternative titles would be suitable for the article? Give reasons for your choice.

a **Keep your own language – but learn another**
b **The spread of English; it's time to fight back**
c **WHY DON'T THE FRENCH LEARN JAPANESE?**

3 According to the writer of the article, are these sentences true (**T**) or false (**F**)?

a Most people are happy to give up their own language and learn a world language.
b Latin used to be a lingua franca.
c Everybody is pleased about the rise of English.
d English people are like elephants.
e If your language dies out, you lose an important part of your culture.
f Multilingualism is a dangerous thing.
g Learning languages can help you to make money.

getting around avoiding (a problem, the truth etc.). "No getting around it" = we can't avoid the fact
identity the unique character of a person/country
lingua franca one language used by various different nationalities to speak to each other
irritates annoys, makes … angry
widespread used in many places/countries
regardless of without considering, it doesn't matter what…
minority a small number of people; ≠ "majority"
novelty new element
reluctance not wanting (to do something)
multilingualism use of two or more languages
dishonored ashamed (AmE spelling)
rivalry competition (to be the most important)
conflict disagreement
vernacular tongue local language (not the official national language)
expanding growing, increasing

Key Language

Look at this sentence from the article.

It is like sleeping next to an elephant.

This is a **simile** – a way of comparing two things using *like*. Similes are very useful if you want to make a point clearly. They can also be funny or poetic.

4 Complete the sentences using these phrases.

- cat food   • a film star   • a computer
- being in prison
- a private cinema   • a bird's nest

a Who does she think she is ? She behaves like ___.
b Ugh! My hair looks like ___!
c They have an enormous television set, like ___.
d I can't eat this. It's like ___.
e You have a brain like ___.
f Living here is like ___.

5 Now make some similes of your own – try to use your imagination!

a Stop behaving like a ___!
b My uncle's house is like ___.
c My sister sings like ___.
d Your eyes are like ___.
e My home town is like ___.
f My friend has ears like ___.

Talk about it

6 Some French speakers in Quebec want independence from English-speaking Canada. The Basque language (Euskera) was banned by the Spanish government; after a long struggle, it was accepted as an official language only in 1980. Why do people care so much about their own language? Would you fight for the right to speak your language?

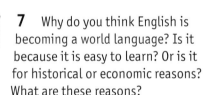

7 Why do you think English is becoming a world language? Is it because it is easy to learn? Or is it for historical or economic reasons? What are these reasons?

8 In some countries people are getting angry about the use of English words in their own language. For example, not everybody likes *le marketing*, *le stress* and *le fast food* in French. How do you feel about this? Does it matter? Can it be stopped?

9 You are learning English at this moment. Is there any other language that you would really like to learn? Give your reasons. Have a vote in your class to discover the most popular language (other than English).

10 There used to be a lot of dialects around Britain – each with its own words and grammatical forms. Now the dialects are more or less dead, and only regional accents remain. Is that a good or a bad thing? Do you speak a dialect? What is happening to dialects in your country?

67

 **Tune in**

1 Before you listen, think about children who are "bilingual", who grow up speaking two languages. Are you bilingual yourself? Would you like to be?

2 Now listen to a conversation between an Asian teenager, Dinesh, and his friend Bina. Fill the gaps with their names.

a ____ is not very good at speaking Hindi.
b ____ told ____ about an uncle's wedding.
c ____'s father is a dentist.
d ____ is about the same in English and Hindi.
e ____ usually speaks English at home.
f ____'s parents speak English to each other.

3 Why does Bina's family switch to Hindi when her grandmother is there?

4 Why do you think Dinesh used Hindi when he talked about his uncle's wedding?

5 How do people in India use English, according to Bina?

 **Key Language**

Look at this sentence from the tape.

> "We quite often switch from one language to the other, depending on the subject."

Can you remember another sentence from the tape with the word **depends** or **depending**?

The two forms have the same meaning. But **depending on**... is part of the same sentence. If you start a new sentence, you have to use **It depends on**... . It's also possible to have another word as the subject.

Example:
The price depends on the size of the memory.

6 Use these words to fill the gaps.

• depends • teacher • it • weather • time • depending

a We play tennis or table-tennis, depending on the ____.
b Our decision ____ on your behaviour.
c I may go or I may stay. ____ depends.
d I can't tell you what we're studying next. It depends on the ____.
e We walk or we take a taxi, depending on how much ____ we have.
f I listen to classical or rock, ____ on how I feel.

Now write sentences which make sense in these contexts.

g ____ . It depends on what the doctor says.
h ____ . It depends on how much money I have.
i ____ . It depends on the temperature of the water.
j ____ . It depends on how good your English is.
k ____ . It depends on what kind of party it is.

LANGUAGE

Over to you

7 Here are some possible effects of growing up bilingual.

a *"After learning two languages, it's easier to learn others."*
b *"When you are very young, you can get confused and speak both languages badly."*
c *"It gives you equal access to two different cultures."*
d *"It upsets older people in the family to see you losing your culture."*
e *"You can get translating or interpreting jobs."*
f *"It gives you a feeling of confidence and power."*
g *"Sometimes it's difficult to decide which language to use - with your friends, for example."*

Decide which are advantages and which are disadvantages. Then work in small groups to choose which you think are the two most important in the list. Finally compare your choices with other groups.

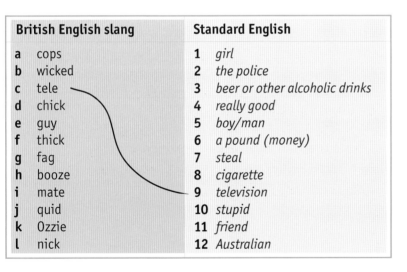

8 In a sense, everybody is bilingual. There are always differences between formal written language and the spoken language you use with friends or family. Give some examples of these differences in your own language.

9 Very informal words are called "slang". Here is a list of some slang words in British English (many of them are different in the USA or Australia). Try to match them with the definitions below.

British English slang	Standard English
a cops	**1** *girl*
b wicked	**2** *the police*
c tele	**3** *beer or other alcoholic drinks*
d chick	**4** *really good*
e guy	**5** *boy/man*
f thick	**6** *a pound (money)*
g fag	**7** *steal*
h booze	**8** *cigarette*
i mate	**9** *television*
j quid	**10** *stupid*
k Ozzie	**11** *friend*
l nick	**12** *Australian*

10 Translate this story into more formal English.

"My mate can be really thick sometimes. He stopped to get some fags and left the car open. He talked to the bird in the shop for about five minutes, and some guy nicked his stereo and two hundred quid from the car. Then he called the cops - but what can they do?"

Write about it

11 Describe the language situation in your country. Is there more than one official language? Are there many different dialects? Are there any political or social problems connected with language?

12 What would it be like if everyone in the world spoke the same language? What would be better or easier? Would we lose anything?

69

NEW TECHNOLOGY

Focus

1 What does the Internet mean to you? Have you ever tried it? Do you think it is a good or a bad thing?

Read about it

Net addicts lead sad virtual lives

by Joe Mathews in Baltimore

In the fall of 1994, Lisa Bowes decided to give up her computer. As an undergraduate in California she'd spent so much time chatting with strangers on the Internet that she eventually made close friends in places as far away as Sweden and Germany. And a man from Pennsylvania she met online came to visit her, with romantic intentions.

Nearly all of her free time – up to seven hours a day – was spent with the computer.

Enough was enough.

"I was definitely an addict," said Ms Bowes, 27. "I met lots of people, but I didn't actually know them. When I decided to give my computer back to my parents, that was really good."

As university students everywhere make greater use of the Internet, some of their lecturers are beginning to worry. Even though the Internet allows for conversations, some students say time on the Net can exaggerate anti-social tendencies and interfere with healthier, face-to-face contact.

One psychologist said he talked with a male college student who, face-to-face, could not ask a woman out. But he had no difficulty doing so over the computer.

Two psychologists at the University of Maryland are even trying to start a support group, Caught In The Net, for those who "find themselves spending too much time on their computers".

But, while some students acknowledge spending up to half of each day on the Net, few believe that heavy use is dangerous.

*The **Guardian**/Baltimore Sun*

2 Write **T** (true) or **F** (false) next to each of these statements.

a Lisa gave up her computer because it was bad for her eyes. **F**
b She wasn't satisfied with the "friends" she made on the Internet. **T**
c She found it difficult to give up the Internet. **T**
d You can have face-to-face contact on the Internet. **F**
e Some people find the Internet easier than real life. **T**
f Caught In The Net is for people who want to learn about the Internet. *most students* **F**

3 According to the article, who is happy about the Internet, and who thinks it may cause problems? *– Some uni. lecturers & psychologists*

addict someone who can't stop (eg. a drug addict)
fall (AmE) autumn
undergraduate university student
exaggerate make bigger/worse
tendencies feelings, parts of your character, which might develop
interfere with damage, make less time for
support group people with one particular problem, who get together to help each other
acknowledge admit, confess

70

Key Language

The Internet has its own language. Before you start using it, you'll need to know a few basic words.

the Net	*the Internet*
virtual	*not real, existing only on the computer*
online	*when you are connected to the Net*
surf	*play with the Net, not looking for anything in particular (the opposite is "search for something")*
download	*copy something from the Net onto your hard disk*
e-mail	*electronic mail: sending letters through the Net*
modem	*the device which connects your computer to the telephone line*

4 Use the words in the list above to fill the gaps in these sentences.

a You find some incredible things when you are ___ing. *surfing*
b I have trouble with the Net because my ___ is not fast enough. *modern*
c I spent two hours ___ searching for that information. *online*
d If you ___ games, you can get a virus in your computer. *download*
e They had a ___ love affair. They never actually met. *virtual*

Talk about it

5 People also get addicted to computer games. Have you played them? Why do you think they are "addictive"?

6 If you collect photos of TV or film stars, or if you study the history of football in South America, the Internet is for you. You can always find groups of people – somewhere in the world – with the same interest or hobby. What special interest groups would you like to check out on the Internet, and why?

7 With television and newspapers, there has always been some government control and censorship. With the Internet, control is almost impossible. Can you think of problems or dangers that might come from the freedom of the Internet?

8 The Internet can offer some wonderful things. For example, how do you think doctors or writers or students might use it? What are the possibilities of the Internet?

1 Before you listen, think about computers. Can you list six different uses of computer technology?

2 Now listen to Mary De Souza, who teaches computer science in an American college. Which two of her examples are illustrated in the photos below? Which other uses does she mention?

3 Mary's father disagrees with her about computers. Listen to the tape again and give her views about these points made by her father.

a *"Supermarkets make more money, but the service is worse for the customer."*
b *"You can't trust computers. They make mistakes."*
c *"Computers have reached the end of the line; there's nothing left for them to do."*
d *"Robots actually cost more than the people which they replace."*
e *"Books are easier to use."*
f *"People still print out most documents, often two or three times."*

Key Language

When you give a list of long examples, how do you introduce each one? Here are some useful phrases.

Introducing examples

- ☐ *Look at...*
- ☐ *And what about...?*
- ☐ *Think about...*
- ☐ *Then there's...*
- ☐ *Take for example...*
- ☐ *Another example is...*

4 Listen to the tape again. Which of these phrases are used by Mary De Souza?

5 Talk about the many uses of plastics in the modern world. Use the phrases to introduce uses in cars, the classroom, sports, electronic equipment. Start like this:

Today, plastics are everywhere. Take for example the kitchen: we have plastic cups and plates, plastic in fridges and microwave ovens.

Over to you

6 Look at this cartoon. Explain the joke to someone who doesn't understand it. Do you think there is a serious point here?

"Dear Santa, What I would like for Christmas. I would like some pens and ink and paper. Also a pencil and a rubber."

7 Computers do some jobs much quicker and cheaper than humans. Make a list of jobs which might be done by computers. Do you think that computers cause unemployment?

8 One CD-ROM can hold the same as almost half a million pages in books. So they are very good for reference materials, like encyclopedias. They can also carry sound and video pictures. But are they better than books in every way? Is there any reason to prefer books?

9 We are in the middle of an "information revolution": computers, CD-ROMs, the Internet and mobile phones. In what ways can these technologies be good for the environment?

Write about it

10 People who cannot speak can now type messages on a computer, and a device called a "voice synthesizer" speaks their words. People with many other disabilities – blindness, deafness, lack of mobility – are helped by computers. Describe a new device which would help a disabled person.

11 A newspaper has organised a competition to win a £2,000 computer. You have to write 200 words about why you need the computer and what you would do with it.

1 In the USA, the number of people with no home – the homeless – has increased a lot in the last few years. Is homelessness a problem in your country?

Read about it

Homeless are run out of town

Every night an army of invisible people disappear into the alleys and abandoned buildings of Austin, Texas. They are the city's homeless.

But here and in more than 40 cities across the United States, the homeless are facing new laws banishing them from the streets. Critics see the movement as proof of the growing hardheartedness of America. There are about 700,000 homeless people in the United States.

In Austin the city council is nearing final approval of a law to ban camping in any public place.

In New Orleans, an anti-camping law has just been proposed, to control the homeless youths who swarm the French Quarter. "The general public is fed up," said New Orleans city council president Peggy Wilson. "People should be able to use public spaces. When other people come in and build cardboard tents and so on, the area becomes inaccessible for everyone else. Particularly in Lafayette Square, there's a group that feeds people on weekends, and they make no effort to clean up; they dump the garbage, and there's the presence of enormous rats."

In Austin, the city's estimated 6,000 homeless can be found near the drinking clubs of Sixth Street, near the University of Texas campus and in tents in corners of the city parks.

It is the business community who wants rid of them most. "Austin is known as an easy city. It provides a lot for the homeless," said Jose Martinez of the Downtown Austin Alliance, which favors the anti-camping bill.

The city's new anti-camping law is expected to carry fines as high as $500. At the same time, the council's homeless task force, is proposing a $3.5 million "campus" for the homeless. Task force member Tom Hatch, an architect, said: "It's insane to make not having a home a crime." *The **Guardian**/Washington Post*

2 "Camping" is usually something you do on holiday. What does it mean in this article?

3 Is it true to say that there are almost three-quarters of a million homeless people in the USA?

4 Which of these are generally "for" (**F**) or "against" (**A**) the homeless?

critics (*paragraph 2*) ☐
the Austin city council (*3*) ☐
the general public (*4*) ☐
Peggy Wilson (*4*) ☐
the group that feeds people (*4*) ☐
the Downtown Austin Alliance (*6*) ☐
the homeless task force (*7*) ☐
Tom Hatch (*7*) ☐

banishing them from   not allowing them on
critics   people who don't agree (with the new law)
hardheartedness   being unkind, cruel
is nearing final approval of   has almost agreed to
ban   prohibit, not allow
swarm   occupy in large numbers (like a "swarm" of bees)
fed up   unhappy
inaccessible   people can't get into, or use, the area
dump   throw away (rubbish)
garbage   (AmE) rubbish
wants rid of them   wants them to go away
downtown   (AmE) city centre
task force   action group (to help the homeless)
campus   university buildings, car parks etc.
   (In paragraph 7, it means a centre built for the homeless)
insane   mad, crazy

Key Language

"Homelessness" is an **abstract noun**. It means "being homeless" or "the idea of being homeless". We can say, for example:

Homelessness is especially bad for children.
Something must be done about homelessness.

You can make many abstract nouns by adding *-ness* to adjectives: *good*→*goodness*
dark→*darkness*
thoughtful→*thoughtfulness*

Be careful! Not all abstract nouns are made in the same way: *stupid*→*stupidity*
intelligent→*intelligence*
cruel→*cruelty*

5 Can you find an abstract noun which ends in *-ness* in the article?

6 Make abstract nouns from the adjectives below (all except one with *-ness*). Then write a short sentence using the noun.

a She is deaf...
    ... but her deafness doesn't stop her working.
b Babies are helpless...
c My father is very mean...

d Don't drive when you're tired...
e These people are poor...
f They were very kind to me...
g Never be late for school...

Talk about it

7 Try to imagine being homeless. How would you feel? What sort of problems would you have? What would you miss most from your present life?

8 In some countries asking for money on the street – "begging" – is illegal. Do you think it should be allowed? Do you ever give money to beggars?

9 Young people can't get a job if they are homeless – and they can't afford a home if they haven't got a job. How can they get out of this dilemma? Should the government or city council do something to help?

10 In Britain some homeless people make money by selling a magazine called *The Big Issue*. Would you buy the magazine? Do you think it's a good idea?

A Big Issue seller

Tune in

1 Before you listen, think about "charities" – organisations which collect money for people who need it. Do you ever give money to them? How do you feel when you give money?

2 Now listen to this argument between Steve and Emily. Steve is collecting money for a charity which helps children in Africa, and Emily is not sure that it's a good idea. What facts on the tape go with each of these numbers?

$50	12 million	20%
15 cents	one million	

Poverty in India

Rich Americans

3 Measles is a virus which gives you little red spots. According to Steve and Emily's conversation, why do American children not normally die of measles?

4 In one sentence, summarise Emily's point of view.

Key Language

5 In a discussion, how do you **disagree politely**, and then make your own point? Which of these phrases did you hear on the tape? Tick (✓) the boxes.

a ☐ No, it won't. But...

b ☐ All right, but...

c ☐ OK, but...

d ☐ That may be true, but...

e ☐ You're right of course. But...

f ☐ I accept that, but...

g ☐ Yes, they do. But...

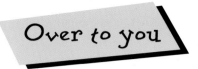

6 Role play. In pairs, act out the parts of Emily and Steve, and continue their argument. Make sure you use some of these phrases from *Key Language*. Spend a few minutes preparing your points before you begin. Here is some information:

Steve

"Unicef says that... "

- half the money spent on cigarettes in Europe would save the lives of all the children in the world who die from preventable disease
- 800 million people in the world do not have enough to eat
- more than 1 billion people do not have clean water
- 25,000 people die each day from diseases carried by dirty water
- half a million babies die each year from tetanus, often because there isn't a clean blade (price: 30 cents) to cut the umbilical cord
- in the poorest countries, life expectancy is only just above 40 years; in the richest countries it is almost 80 years

Emily

"In the USA... "

- there are about 700,000 homeless people, including 100,000 children
- there is a lot of unemployment. When the City of Los Angeles advertised for 100 low-paid cleaners, 25,000 people applied
- every day six children commit suicide, most of them from poor families
- all around us there are adverts showing rich people enjoying expensive products
- getting rich is part of the "American Dream"

7 How do you feel about the role of charities? Is it a good way to help the poor, or should the government deal with such problems?

8 One famous type of sports shoe is made in Pakistan and costs $70 to buy in the USA. But who exactly gets the money?

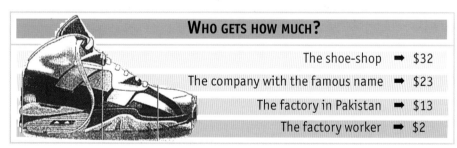

WHO GETS HOW MUCH?	
The shoe-shop	➡ $32
The company with the famous name	➡ $23
The factory in Pakistan	➡ $13
The factory worker	➡ $2

9 Rich countries pay very low prices for goods from poor countries – not only factory-made things, but also fruit, vegetables, coffee etc.. Is this right? What can be done about it?

10 Write a letter to the chief executive of a famous sports-shoe company. Tell her/him how you feel about the statistics in the chart above.

11 Imagine you are a beggar. Write a diary for one day of your life on the streets.

12 Choose a charity organisation that you would like to work for. Write a letter to be sent out to millions of people. Ask for money and explain why they should give some to your organisation.

1 Is racism a problem in your country? What recent examples of racism have you read or heard about?

Read about it

Arrest of black lecturer heightens distrust

Michael Leary had arranged to meet his friend at 8pm outside McDonald's in Brixton, South London.

Dressed in smart casual clothes Mr Leary, 39, waited for about 20 minutes. He wandered down the busy street. There was no sign of her, so he returned to his spot outside the fast food store.

At 8.30pm two white men approached him. Mr Leary is black. The men, plain-clothed police officers, said they had seen him "hanging around" and were going to take him to Brixton police station to search him for drugs.

"I was completely shocked," recalled Mr Leary. "I told them I was waiting for a friend, and I was a university lecturer. They started pushing and pulling me around. When I refused to take my hands out of my pockets, the youngest officer got

the handcuffs and forced them on me. They hurt my wrist."

Three police cars and a van arrived. "I was pushed into a car. I said there was no need to use force and one of the officers told me to "shut up" as if I was a piece of dirt."

He was taken to Brixton police station, where he claims he was "pulled" along by his handcuffs "like a cow". He was told to take off his clothes so that he could be searched.

No drugs were found. His credit cards were taken to see whether they were stolen.

There was no apology or explanation. "I was arrested and searched because I was a black man in Brixton. I was just waiting for a friend and minding my own business, but I was made to feel like a criminal."

THE INDEPENDENT

2 Re-tell the story by putting these sentences in the right order.

a He walked down the street to see if his friend was there. ☐
b He returned to McDonald's. ☐
c He waited for 20 minutes. ☐
d He was approached by two policemen. ☐
e Michael arrived outside McDonald's. ☐
f He was handcuffed. ☐
g He was searched and, finally, released. ☐
h He was taken away in a car. ☐

3 Which one of these headlines would be suitable for the article? Explain why the others would *not* be suitable.

a **Police say sorry to black lecturer**

b **Lecturer accuses police of racism**

c **UNIVERSITY LECTURER FOUND WITH DRUGS**

lecturer university teacher
casual not formal, eg. a pullover and jeans, not a suit and tie
wandered walked slowly
spot place, position
plain-clothed not in uniform (working but pretending to be members of the public)
hanging around being in a place, but not doing anything particular
search look in pockets, shoes etc.
handcuffs metal rings which police use when arresting somebody
minding my own business not interfering with anybody

Key Language

Look at this sentence from the article.

> The men, plain-clothed police officers, said they had seen him "hanging around"…

4 In written English we often put extra information (**"plain-clothed police officers"**) between commas. Can you find another example in the article?

5 When speaking, we usually make extra sentences, as in **a–h** below. Put two sentences together to make one, with information between commas.

a Dave's a tennis player. He has two children.
   Dave, a tennis player, has two children.

b George Bush is coming to speak at the conference next week. He's the ex-President of the USA.

c Ms Santoni is 23. She is a candidate in the general election.

d Hong Kong was once a British colony. It is now a city in China.

e Soccer is now the most popular international sport in the world. It started in England almost 200 years ago.

f Bill Gates started his career as a software writer. He is the richest man in the world.

g The *"Mona Lisa"* (*"La Gioconda"*) was painted by the Italian Leonardo da Vinci. It is now in the Louvre in Paris.

Talk about it

6 The police in Britain use "identity codes" (*i/c's*) when they are describing people. For example *i/c1* means "white", *i/c2* means Mediterranean, *i/c3* means black. If they say "male i/c3, mid-teens", they mean "black boy, about 15 years old". Do you think it is right to use these racial descriptions? Why/why not?

7 Some people are embarrassed to talk about race. They think it might be offensive to others. How do you feel? Should we talk about it, or is it better to keep quiet?

8 The National Front is a racist political party in Britain. It wants to "send back" black and Asian people to "where they came from". Do you have parties like this in your country? Why do some people support them?

9 In the USA, they have tried to increase the numbers of black people in some jobs by "positive action". If a white person and a black person have the same qualifications, the black person gets the job. Is this a good idea?

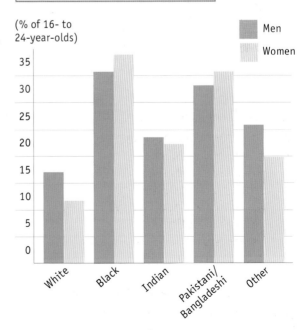

Youth unemployment rates
Averages for May 1995 – May 1996

(% of 16- to 24-year-olds)

10 What does the table above tell us? What could be the reasons for the differences between the various groups?

Tune in

1 Before you listen, think about what it is like to marry someone of a different race. What sort of obstacles would you expect to face?

2 Listen to Tarik and Katie talking about their marriage. Which of them experienced more resistance from members of the family?

3 What did Katie's grandparents really mean when they said "You're too young to settle down"?

4 Write **T** (true) or **F** (false) next to each of these statements.

a Katie feels that there's a lot of racism in Camden. ☐
b Katie was an only child. ☐
c Katie's parents were more positive than her grandparents. ☐
d Tarik's grandmother can't speak English. ☐
e Tarik and Katie are planning to have children. ☐
f Tarik's family are now happier about the marriage. ☐

Key Language

Look at this sentence from the tape.

"What upset me was the attitude of my grandparents."

Katie could also use a simpler sentence – "The attitude of my grandparents upset me".
But she uses **What...** to change the focus. It puts emphasis on **"the attitude of my grandparents"**.

5 Can you remember another sentence in this form on the tape?

6 Change these sentences into the *What...* form.
a They're looking for a place with friendly people.
  What they're looking for is a place with friendly people.
b I really hate hypocrisy.
c The attitude of your neighbours is very important.
d Love for their grandchildren changed their views.
e Racism makes life difficult in some parts of London.
f Pressure from the family separates a lot of couples.

Over to you

7 Marriage between people of different races, a "mixed marriage", was forbidden under "apartheid" in South Africa, and by the Nazis in Germany. Why do you think these racist regimes were so opposed to it?

8 If your parents come from two different cultures, do you feel you are outside both cultures? Or do you benefit from being a part of both?

9 What might be the positive effects of "mixed marriages" for society?

10 Would a difference of religion stop you marrying someone? How can couples overcome this difference?

11 Some communities, like the Indians in Britain, stay close together and preserve their identity – with language, food, religion, music etc.. Would it be better for them to integrate more quickly into British society?

12 Generally, as time goes on, ethnic groups integrate into the wider community. But some black people in the USA, like Louis Farrakhan of "Nation of Islam", want to go in the opposite direction – to become more separate. Can you understand this attitude? Do you agree with it?

Louis Farrakhan

Write about it

13 Imagine you are Michael Leary, the black lecturer who was arrested in Brixton. Write a letter of complaint to the Metropolitan (London) police. Start like this:

Dear Chief Constable,
I wish to complain about the behaviour of your officers in a recent incident...

14 Write a newspaper article describing race relations in the area where you live. How do different ethnic groups feel about each other? If there are problems, what can be done?

1 Do you know anyone who has left home?
Why did they leave? Did they go back home eventually?

Read about it

This is an extract from a journal kept by the mother of a 17-year-old girl who left home

Diary of a walkout

March 10. Kate demands money for getting ears pierced. I refuse. Cries, threatens, bangs on my bedroom door, then: *You're so unsupportive, you don't talk to me nicely any more. There's no point in my staying.* Slam.

March 14. Appears with former boyfriend to collect belongings. Watching her stuff clothes in bag causes me almost physical pain.

March 18. She's moved out of former boyfriend's house, left school. No-one knows where she is.

March 26. Search area where I know she hangs out. Spot her standing in a doorway smoking. Take her for coffee. She tells me she's staying with Melanie. Won't divulge phone number.

March 30. Volunteers phone number – *just don't think you can ring me all the time.*

April 7. Melanie's dad says Kate has to move out. Suggest she comes home. Doesn't work. She disappears again.

April 12. Hear she's living in a boarding house with a friend.

April 14. She makes contact and I meet her for dinner. Says the room in the boarding house needs a good clean. We go shopping for bleach, detergent and food.

April 16. My birthday. A bouquet arrives on my doorstep with a note: *No matter what I do, Mum, I love you.*

April 18. Rings to say she accepted a lift from a man at 2 am today, was attacked, but managed to get out of the car. Feel scared, helpless.

April 20. Moves out of the boarding house to another "friend" on the other side of the city.

April 23. It's 3 am and she's on the phone crying, saying the "friend" is throwing her out. The phone goes dead and I have no idea where she is.

April 30. Moves into a flat with a friend. Asks for rent money. Agree to pay one month's rent, but no more – she has to get a job.

May 30. Is evicted from her flat. Cautiously suggest she returns home for a day or two and uses phone to find alternative accommodation and job. Grudgingly agrees. *I'll be outta here by the end of the week.*

Six months later. She's nicer to live with, has gone back to school. Overhear her talking on the phone discussing a friend who has walked out of home. *Silly bitch. Tell her to grow up and move back*

The Sydney Morning Herald

2 Put the events of the story in their correct order **1–9.**

a Her mother gives her rent money. ☐

b Kate shouts at her mother and leaves home. ☐

c She and an old boyfriend come back to collect her things. ☐

d She comes home for a few days. ☐

e She goes to stay with Melanie for a while. ☐

f She is thrown out of the flat. ☐

g She moves in with a friend on the other side of the city. ☐

h She moves into a boarding house. ☐

i She's still living at home six months later. ☐

walkout (here) person who leaves home after a fight
get ears pierced have holes put in ears for earrings
former previous
belongings things
stuff push quickly and carelessly
hangs out spends time
spot notice
divulge tell
boarding house a place that rents out cheap rooms
no matter what whatever
scared frightened
throwing her out telling her to leave
evicted told to leave
accommodation place to stay
grudgingly without enthusiasm
outta out of (slang)
bitch an offensive way to describe a girl/woman ("bitch" = a female dog)
grow up be more mature

Key Language

Read this sentence from the article.

> [She] won't divulge [the] phone number.

The phrase **won't** do something means *refuses to do* something. The past tense is **wouldn't**.
Examples:
I've advised her to come home but she won't listen.
He wouldn't complete his studies; he dropped out of school at sixteen.

3 Rewrite these sentences using *won't* or *wouldn't*.

a He refuses to get a job and earn his own living.
   He won't get a job and earn his own living.

b Kate's mother refused to give her money to get her ears pierced.

c She refuses to conform.

d She refused to give her more than one month's rent.

e Many teenagers walk out because their parents refuse to listen to them.

f Why does he refuse to think about the future?

4 The phrasal verbs in the box below are used in the article. Complete each sentence with the correct one.

- move out of
- hang out
- get out
- throw out
- walk out

a These are the rules of the house and if you don't like them you can just ___ now.

b At the weekends I get up late then go and ___ with my friends.

c We're going to ___ this flat at the end of the month because it's too expensive for us.

d A growing number of teenagers ___ of home each year, after a fight with their parents.

e Her school has threatened to ___ her ___ if she skips classes again.

Talk about it

5 What is special about the diary style of writing used in the article? Talk about: personal pronouns, possessive adjectives and direct speech.

6 Roleplay a conversation between Kate and her old boyfriend after Kate walks out. Start like this:
KATE: "I've had a row with my mother and I've left."
BOYFRIEND: "What do you mean, you've left?"

7 Do you think Kate was right to leave home? Why/why not?

8 When does Kate make contact with her mother?
What does Kate seem to want from her relationship with her mother?
Money? Support? Friendship? Emotional reactions? Advice?

9 This is a list of the most common reasons why teenagers walk out.

- Teenager needs to establish own identity
- Teenager feels under pressure about the future
- Parent doesn't listen or doesn't care
- Violence at home
- Parent is strict
- Parent's expectations are too high
- Teenager can't accept one parent's new partner

Which of them do you think made Kate walk out? Which four reasons would be/would have been most likely to make you leave home? Discuss your decision with a partner.

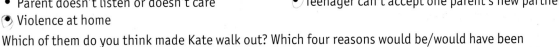

Tune in

1 List three cult figures of your generation. Why are they popular? Are any of them rebels?

2 You are going to hear a biography of Kurt Cobain, lead singer of the American rock band Nirvana. Before you listen, read the information below. As you listen, complete the chart.

Feb 20th 1967	Kurt Cobain was born.
At 8	His parents ____ .
In his teens	Experimented with ____ .
At 18	Dropped out of ____ .
19___	Nirvana was formed.
1989	Their first album, *Bleach*, ____ .
1991	Second album, *Nevermind,* was a big ____ . The sound was a ____ of punk and rock. People called it "grunge". Kurt and Courtney Love ____ .
1992	Kurt and Courtney's baby ____ . Third album, ____ , came out.
1993	*In Utero*, their fourth album, came out. Kurt continued to take drugs.
April 5th___	Kurt ____ . Last words: *"Remember it's better to burn out than fade away."*

Key Language

The verbs **look for**, **look after** and **look out** have very different meanings. Verbs like these are called **phrasal verbs**.

Examples:
I'm looking for my keys. I can't find them anywhere.
Please look after my dog while I'm on holiday.
Look out! Don't sit on the photographs.

3 Listen to the tape again and complete the phrasal verbs. Then match them to the meanings.

a	drop ____ (of)	1	*appear*
b	come ____	2	*become a couple*
c	smash ____	3	*break*
d	____ together (with)	4	*die gradually*
e	get ____	5	*release*
f	bring ____	6	*ruin your health at a young age*
g	give ____	7	*stop attending*
h	burn ____	8	*stop taking*
i	fade ____	9	*stop taking*

4 Use the notes in Exercise 2 and the phrasal verbs in Exercise 3 to retell Kurt Cobain's life story. Work in pairs. Take turns saying one sentence each.

Over to you

5 "Rebels usually prefer rock music to classical or folk music". Do you agree?

6 Do you have the same taste as your parents in music, TV programmes, people, fashion? Do you share their political views? If not, do you consider yourself rebellious, or simply independent?

7 Do you ever wish you could rebel? What situations make you feel like this? What rebellious action would you like to take? Give a one minute speech on the subject.

8 Roleplay a conversation between two friends. One of them wants to drop out of school. The other is advising against it.

Write about it

9 Describe the most rebellious person you know. What sort of clothes does s/he wear? What sort of music does s/he like? What sort of things has s/he done? Do you admire him/her? Why/why not?

10 In his teens, Kurt Cobain was arrested for doing graffiti on the wall of a bank. He had written *Homosex Rules* because he had a close friend who was homosexual. And one of his guitars carried the slogan *Vandalism: Beautiful As A Rock In A Cop's Face*. Write some slogans that you would like to see in public places. Explain why you would like to write them.

Focus

1 In your country, is it easy for a woman to become a manager? If not, why do you think it is difficult for a woman to get to the top?

Read about it

THE CONCRETE CEILING

Why women are up against it

Someone once observed that a glass ceiling blocks women's rise to the top. But it seems more like a concrete ceiling. The following could be what's stopping us:

 Because boys are taken more seriously than girls at school.

 Because some female high achievers, such as Margaret Thatcher, often don't promote other women.

 Because women have babies.

 Because men think women won't be as committed to their job once they have a child.

 Because "women get all moody and useless once a month".

 Because a woman is still judged on her looks.

 Because women think men won't love them any more if they're successful.

 Because women are busy doing housework when they could be training, impressing the boss and networking.

 Because "women's brains are smaller".

 Because working mothers are made to feel guilty.

 Because women are told to start out as secretaries, and good secretaries rarely get promoted.

 Because not enough women have the courage or confidence to speak out about inequality.

 Because women say sorry, sorry, sorry all the time.

 Because women are either too tough or not tough enough.

 Because men fear and distrust powerful women.

 Because no one ever thinks of calling the father when a child is ill.

 Because a lot of men genuinely think of themselves as superior to women.

 Because some men just don't listen to what women are saying.

 Just because.

---

up against it facing problems
glass ceiling an invisible barrier which stops you going up
high achievers very successful people
committed dedicated, hardworking
moody changeable (happy, sad, calm, angry etc.)

looks appearance, eg. pretty, ugly
networking meeting other people in your business, making useful contacts
promoted given a better/higher job in a company
tough (negative idea) aggressive; (positive idea) strong

2 Look again at the article. Which sentences have almost the same meaning as these?

a When a child has a problem, people refer to the mother first.

b Successful women should show more solidarity with other women.

c Women apologise too much.

d If you are at the bottom of a company, you will probably stay at the bottom.

e Women are either weak or aggressive.

f To be successful, women have to be pretty.

g Women with children don't work so hard at the office (according to men).

Key Language

Look at this sentence from the article.

> Because boys are taken more seriously than girls at school.

The verb phrase ***are taken*** is the **passive** form. The **active** would be:

Teachers take boys more seriously than girls at school.

Why do we use the passive here? Because the most important point is about "boys" and "girls", not "teachers". In a passive sentence you can leave out the subject of the active sentence if it is not important.

3 Can you find any more passive forms in the article? (One of them uses *get* instead of *is/are*.)

4 Put these active sentences into the passive. Leave out the subjects (in brackets).

a (People) don't always respect women managers.
  Women managers aren't always respected.

b (People) expect women to do the housework.

c (People) judge women and men by different standards.

d (Companies) promote men much more quickly.

e (Men) fear and distrust powerful women.

f (Companies) often keep the best jobs for men.

g (Teachers) give more time to boys in the classroom.

Talk about it

5 Can you think of another title for the article, without using the expressions "glass ceiling" or "concrete ceiling"?

6 Some of the sentences in the article could be categorised Men's Attitudes. Find five examples. Then find four sentences for the category Childcare and Housework.

7 Which are the most important points in the article? Choose the top three and explain them in your own words.

8 Invent two more sentences beginning "Because..." to add to the article. Discuss them with your partner.

 **Tune in**

1 Before you listen, do a survey in your class. Do any of you know women who are studying or who have studied a scientific subject at university?

2 Now listen to Sandra Herzog, who is studying physics at MIT (Massachusetts Institute of Technology) in Boston, USA. Look at the pictures below. Which things are mentioned?

3 Listen to the tape again, and complete the chart below with information about the way Sandra and her brothers were treated.

	Sandra	her brothers
gifts		
extra lessons		*math tuition*
activities with parents		
parents' ambitions for them		

4 Now answer these questions about Sandra and her family.

a What were Sandra's parents' jobs?
b What did her parents think about a scientific career?
c How is Sandra getting on with her university course?

Key Language

5 Match these words from the tape with their definitions.

a stereotyping
b housewife
c ambitions
d support
e equal opportunities
f sexist

1 thinking one sex is inferior to the other
2 the same rights for women and men
3 help, encouragement
4 what you want to do, be, have in the future
5 (here) thinking all girls are the same
6 woman who does not go out to work

6 Complete these sentences from the tape with words from Question 5.

a They have always had lots of ___ from my parents.
b My dad's a doctor, and my mom's a ___ .
c For me, ___ is an important idea.
d I think the ___ began when we were little kids.
e I guess they had the same ___ for their children.

7 Think about women who have successful careers. Choose one - it could be a member of your family, a friend, or a famous woman you know about. Tell your group about her. Has she succeeded in a man's world? Does she also look after a family? What about particular problems she might have in her career? Has she experienced sexist attitudes from men, or even from other women?

8 What is your reaction to this picture? Do you feel the same about male bodybuilders? Do you think that bodybuilding is a good thing for women? Give reasons for your answer.

9 Which of these sports are usually for men rather than women?

badminton	athletics	football
baseball tennis	boxing	motor-racing
swimming rugby	skiing	sumo wrestling

Are the men's sports in the list equally suitable for women? Makes notes and then discuss your reasons in a group.

10 Role play in pairs. One of you is the director of a big computer company, the other is a trade union representative. Discuss ways to make it easier for women to get promotion in the company.
These ideas may help you:

- creche at the office?
- maternity leave?
- attitudes of present managers?
- equal opportunities?
- flexible working hours?
- extra training?

Write about it

11 You are a bored housewife with a working husband and two small children. You are treated like an unpaid servant. You'd like to have your own career.

Write a letter to the problem page of a magazine. Talk about your life and ask for advice. Start like this:

Dear Claire,
I have to do something to change my life in some way. Every day I...

12 Give parents some advice on how to avoid "stereotyping" when they bring up their daughters and sons. Write six points like this example:

"Don't give boys more attention than girls, even if they want it."

Focus

1 Have you done any of the sports illustrated on this page? Would you like to try any of them? Why/why not?

Read about it

Slobbing is good for you

Not only is being a couch potato an enjoyable way to spend your days, it could also mean you have more days to enjoy. Yes, professional couching is good for your health and may increase your lifespan. Here are the facts:
- An average of 19 million sports related injuries are reported every year in England and Wales alone.
- According to the Office for National Statistics, 84 people died of sporting injuries in one recent year. And that doesn't include the 58 who drowned.
- Bungee-jumping has resulted in a new type of back and neck strain. Mountaineering and air sports such as hang-gliding, each kill at least 16 people every year. In Japan, skiing is the greatest source of sport-related death and impact injury. A Harvard Medical School doctor even reported 11 cases of strangulation of skiers wearing long scarves.
- In one Sports Council study of 28,000 people, soccer was found responsible for more than a quarter of 2000 injuries seen every month.
- Rugby is three times more dangerous than the next most risky activities: soccer, field hockey, cricket and the martial arts.
- The New England Journal of Medicine reported on 25 sportsmen killed when they were hit on the chest over the heart with a ball or hockey puck. It is thought that such a blow triggers a fatal upset to the rhythm of the heart beat.
- New sports injuries cost the NHS at least £240 million each year.
- Scientific evidence suggests that prolonged, strenuous training can impair the immune system, reducing the body's ability to fight infection. Athletes fall ill more often than couch potatoes. So lie back and enjoy yourself.

F H M

2 Complete the following sentences with these numbers from the box.

16	**a** Every year ___ sports injuries are reported in England and Wales.
19 million	**b** In one recent year, there were ___ deaths from sports injuries.
84	**c** Every year ___ people die in air sports, and the same number die mountaineering.
240 million	**d** The Sports Council did a survey of ___ people. It showed that ___ people per month
500	got hurt playing football.
28,000	**e** In Britain, medical treatment for new sports injuries costs more than ___ pounds per ye

---

slobbing being very lazy
couch potato person who sits (often on a sofa - "couch") and watches TV all day
couching being a couch potato
lifespan the length of your life
drowned died in the water because they were unable to breathe
bungee-jumping jumping from a very high point with feet attached to a long piece of rubber

hang-gliding flying while attached to a large kite
impact injury damage to the body when in direct contact with somebody/something
strangulation death from lack of respiration caused by something tight around the neck
risky dangerous
martial arts eg. karate and aikido

hockey puck flat piece of rubber used instead of a ball in ice hockey
triggers starts
upset to change in
NHS National Health Service, the British system of free medical treatment
strenuous very heavy
impair weaken
immune system the body's method of fighting diseases

Key Language

Read these sentences from the article.

> ... it could also mean you have more days to enjoy.
> Couching ... may increase your lifespan.

We use **could**, **may** and **might** to say that something is a possibility.
The negative is **mightn't** or **may not**, not **couldn't**.

Example:
*She **mightn't** win the race. She **might** come second.*

may not	may
~~couldn't~~	could

3 Match the prompts **a-g** to the results. Then make sentences with **should** and **could**, **may not**, **might(n't)**.

Example:
You should warm up before you run or you could pull a muscle.

a	warm up before you run	**1**	feel stiff the next day
b	stretch after exercising	**2**	get a tooth broken
c	wear goggles when you swim	**3**	get sore eyes
d	never dive into water you don't know	**4**	injure your feet
e	wear a mouth guard for football	**5**	not finish the course
f	practise regularly before a marathon	**6**	pull a muscle
g	wear good trainers	**7**	water not be very deep

Talk about it

4 What is the point of the article? Who is it talking to?
Do you think the article could persuade somebody to give up sport?

5 What sports do you do? How regularly do you do them? Have you ever been injured doing sport or exercise? What happened? What do you do to prevent injury?

6 What do you think are the most dangerous sports? Do you do any of them? Why/why not?

7 Put the following benefits of sport in order of importance with **1** as the most important. Discuss your answers with a partner. Do a class survey to compare results.

> makes your body more flexible   increases strength
> increases stamina   tones the muscles
> helps you to relax   good way of meeting people
> allows you to get rid of aggression
> good for competitive instinct   teaches you to be part of a team

1 Before you listen, make a list of the worst aspects of professional sport.

2 Now listen to three people talking about professional sport and tick (✓) the criticisms made by the speakers.

a The best players retire from sport too early.

b Local football teams lose their best players to top clubs.

c There's too much sport on TV.

d Ticket prices for football matches are too high.

e There's a lot of drug taking in sport.

f The top games aren't shown on free TV stations.

g There's too much pressure on young sports people.

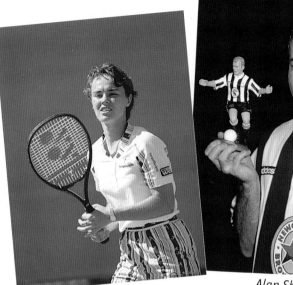

Martina Hingis   *Alan Shearer*

3 Listen again and complete these sentences.

a *"Top clubs pay ___ up to a million pounds a year."*

b *"The best players play for the team that pays ___ the ___."*

Key Language

Read the sentences in Exercise 3 again.

Some verbs like **pay** can have two objects: a **direct object** and an **indirect object**.

They paid the money to the cashier.
or
They paid the cashier the money.

Here are some more verbs which can take two objects:

- give • tell • show
- lend • offer • send

Can you think of any others?

4 Complete each sentence with the correct word or phrase.

- some money • me • that joke
- the police • to everyone

a Who told you ___?

b My brother told it ___.

c We showed ___ the broken window.

d We must give this information ___.

e They offered ___ some tickets to the match.

f He lent me ___ to buy a football shirt.

g We sent the invitations ___ last week.

Over to you

5 In one season, American basketballer, Michael Jordan, makes $30 million and baseball's Albert Belle makes $10 million. Do you think professional athletes' salaries are too high?

6 Why do some athletes use steroids and other drugs? Is it possible to stop drug use in sport? If you were a top athlete would you take drugs to improve your performance?

7 Football is the most popular spectator sport in Europe. In America, baseball and basketball are the most popular. What is your favourite spectator sport? What do you like about it?

8 Fishing and walking are the most popular "sporting" activities in Europe. Do you think they are sports? Why/why not?

9 Why are jogging, aerobics and working out in the gym so popular?

10 Do you think boxing should be banned? Why/why not?

Michael Jordan

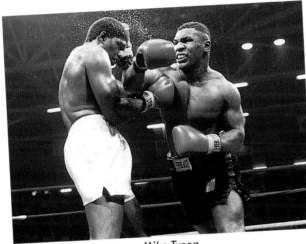
Mike Tyson

Write about it

11 Write a letter to a foreign friend describing a recent sporting event you watched. Say where it took place, who you went with, what sort of match it was, why you went, whether or not you enjoyed it and who won. Start like this:

> Dear ___,
> There was a ___ match/tournament in/at ___ recently and I went to see it with ___. We arrived at the stadium/pitch/gym at...

12 Write a dialogue between two friends. One friend does a lot of sport and is trying to persuade his/her friend, who never does sport, to take it up. Start:

A: *I'm thinking of going for a run this evening. Would you like to come with me?*

B: *No, thanks, ___. You know I hate running!*

Daily Mail

Over 2.2 million copies of the The Daily Mail are sold every day. The paper has won many awards for its campaigning, its news reports, special features and design. *For Internet information: www.dailymail.co.uk*

The Daily Telegraph

The Daily Telegraph is the best-selling of the four "quality" British newspapers (the others are The Times, The Guardian and The Independent), selling over one million copies a day. The newspaper was first published in 1855.
For Internet information: www.Telegraph.co.uk

Evening Standard

Founded in 1827 and now London's only evening newspaper, The Evening Standard focuses on the top news stories that will be in the national newspapers the next day. Nearly half a million copies are sold throughout the day – from the first edition at 9 am to the "evening final".
For Internet information: www.standard.co.uk

The Guardian

The Guardian, which started in 1821, has a daily circulation of over 400,000. It often prints articles in translation from important European newspapers.
For Internet information: www.guardian.co.uk

THE INDEPENDENT

The Independent is a British daily newspaper which was launched in 1986. It is noted for its photojournalism and offers a mixture of news stories ("busy" pages) and longer articles/features ("long reads").
For Internet information: www.independent.co.uk

Herald International Tribune

The International Herald Tribune is a daily newspaper. Its headquarters are in Paris and it is printed in 14 cities. Started in 1887, the IHT focuses on international political and business news. Around 208,000 copies are sold daily to over 180 countries.
For Internet information: www.iht.com

The Observer

The Observer is the oldest Sunday newspaper in the world. It was first published in 1791. Like its rival The Sunday Times, it has many sections which focus on world news, sport, arts, business and finance. Its weekly circulation is around 450,000.
For Internet information: www.guardian.co.uk

THE SUNDAY TIMES

The Sunday Times was started in 1821. The paper is world-famous for its investigative journalism and its news and business reports. The Sunday Times has many different sections covering news, business, sport, fashion, arts and entertainment. Around 1,350,000 copies are sold every week.
For Internet information: www.sunday-times.co.uk

The Sydney Morning Herald

The Sydney Morning Herald is Australia's oldest publication (it was founded in 1831) and also its leading newspaper. It has a daily circulation of 270,000 and focuses on local, national and international issues, with special emphasis on Asia.
For Internet information: www.smh.com.au

CHILDREN'S EXPRESS
BY CHILDREN FOR EVERYONE

Children's Express is a British news agency run by young people aged 8-18. This charity was started in Britain in 1995 and has two bureaux: London and Newcastle (in the northeast of England). Children's Express aims to "give young people a voice in the media". Over 50 articles are published every year in local and national newspapers.
For Internet information: www.ce.org

COSMOPOLITAN

Cosmopolitan is a monthly magazine for women, published in various international editions, which "addresses the issues that all women face – in love, or work, and in the world". Its UK edition sells over 406,000 copies every month,
For Internet information: www.cosmomag.com

FHM

FHM is For Him Magazine, a full-colour magazine for men with features on famous people, fashion, health, food and travel.
For Internet information: www.erack,com/fhm

Forbes

Forbes is an American weekly magazine with features on business, finance, law and technology. Its focus is national and international.
For Internet information: www.forbes.com

FRIENDS *of the* **earth**

Friends of the Earth, one of the UK's leading pressure groups, focuses on protecting and improving the environment, present and future.
For Internet information:www.foe.co.uk

livewire

Livewire is an onboard rail magazine "to entertain and inform" people travelling on trains in Britain. It publishes features on celebrities as well as focussing on business news and other "human interest" stories.

New Woman

New Woman is a magazine which targets working women aged 25-34. It features articles on fashion, fitness, health and psychology, as well as focusing on beauty photojournalism. Over a quarter of a million copies of the magazine are sold every month.
For Internet information: www.erack.com/nwoman

Newsweek

This full-colour American weekly magazine was launched in 1933. It focuses on political affairs and news stories covering the USA and Asia.
For Internet information: www.newsweek.com

19

19 is a British monthly magazine for women (aged 19) with features on Life, Style and Entertainment.
For Internet information: www.19@co.uk

U.S.News

This colour magazine sells more than two million copies a week in the United States. U.S. News & World Report focuses on national and international news, as well as publishing features on business, science and technology.
For Internet information: www.usnews.com

KEY
(*adj*) = adjective
(*adv*) = adverb
(*coll*) = colloquial
(*n*) = noun
(*np*) = noun phrase
(*phr v*) = phrasal verb
(*sl*) = slang
(*v*) = verb
(*vp*) = verb phrase
(*AmE*) = American English
≠ = opposite of

• The page numbers refer to the first example of the word/phrase in the book.

abandoned (*adj*) 74 empty
absent (*adj*) 62 not here/not there
activist (*n*) 10 someone who works hard for a social or political idea
addict (*n*) 36 someone who cannot stop doing something (eg. taking drugs) [*n* = **addiction**]
additives (*n*) 52 chemicals added to food (eg. to make them stay fresh longer)
aerobics (*n*) 93 exercise done in a class with music
affair (*n*) 26 situation; 41 sexual relationship – usually secret – between two people not married to each other
afterlife (*n*) 24 life after death (eg. in heaven or hell)
aggression (*n*) 91 feeling of anger
aggressive (*adj*) 18 angry (≠ shy)
agnostic (*n*) 24 person who believes that it is impossible to know anything about God or life after death
alley (*n*) 74 very small, narrow street
alternative (*adj*) 66 other, different

ammunition (*n*) 77 ideas to use in an argument
apartheid (*n*) 81 old system in South Africa: whites and blacks lived and worked separately
appearance (*n*) 18 looks
argue (*v*) 17 fight
arrest (*v*) 16 catch (eg. "The police **arrested** the thief.")
astrology (*n*) 24 the study of how the stars and planets influence people's lives
atheist (*n*) 24 person who does not believe in God
atmosphere (*n*) 38 the feeling in a place
attend (*v*) 25 go to, watch
attitude (*n*) 14 what you think/feel about something

background (*n*) 46 sounds you can hear but you are not listening to
ban (*v*) 30 forbid, make illegal
behaviour (*n*) 26 way of acting
bizarre (*adj*) 10 strange
blame (*v*) 42 think someone/ something causes a situation
bleach (*n*) 82 product used for cleaning/making clothes whiter/making hair lighter
blindness (*n*) 73 not being able to see
break free (*v*) 42 escape from rules
brilliant (*adj*) 14 very good, very clever
bring up (*v*) 89 look after/ educate (eg. "Parents **bring up** their children.")
broadcast (*n*) 13 a radio/TV programme

Camembert (*n*) 66 a type of French cheese
candidate (*n*) 28 politician who tries to win an election

capacity (*n*) 66 "in that capacity" = for that use/ purpose
cardboard (*n*) 74 thick, hard paper (boxes are made of it)
catastophe (*n*) 58 disaster
cautiously (*adv*) 82 carefully
censor (*v*) 49 cut parts of films/TV programmes
character (*n*) 18 personality, qualities
charge (*v*) 63 ask for money
charity (*n*) 62 organisation that helps poor people
chat (*v*) 70 talk to people for fun – not about important things
cheat (*v*) 63 behave dishonestly in order to do better (eg. in an exam) or to win (eg. at cards, in sport)
checked (*adj*) 18 clothes which have a pattern of squares
chief executive (*np*) 77 boss, top person in a company
claim (*v*) 23 say something which might not be true
clerk (*n*) 28 (*AmE*) shop assistant
colourants (*n*) 52 chemicals added to food to change its colour
comforting (*adj*) 18 making someone feel happier
commercial (*n*) 7 advert on TV/radio or at the cinema
competitive (*adj*) 43 wanting to prove that s/he is the best; enjoying competition
competitive instinct (*np*) 91 wanting to win a competition
concentrated (*adj*) 50 found in the largest amounts
concrete (*n*) 86 mixture (cement, sand, water and small stones) used for buildings
confidence (*n*) 69 feeling good about yourself
confidential (*adj*) 35 not public (eg. doctor's records)

conform (v) 83 be like other people

confused (adj) 69 not clear in your mind

consideration (n) 50 thing to worry about

constantly (adv) 42 always

consume (v) 52 eat

contraception (n) 24 birth control; ways of preventing pregnancy

contract (v) 10 get (an illness or disease)

contribute (v) 58 add (to do something good or to a problem)

corporal punishment (np) 33 physical punishment (eg. hitting)

courage (n) 86 strength

create (v) 35 make, produce

creche (n) 89 place where very small children can be left and looked after

credit card (np) 78 plastic card for buying things (eg. American Express card)

cricket (n) 90 outdoor game similar to baseball, popular in Britain

critic (n) 15 someone who writes in the newspaper about art, books, films etc.

criticise (v) 23 say bad things (about)

cult figure (np) 84 person who is very popular (eg. leader of a fashion in music, art, writing) among a small group of people

culture (n) 38 all the particular things about a country/a people: religion, music, food, customs etc.

currently (adv) 14 now, at the moment

customer (n) 72 person who buys goods/services (eg. from a shop)

 D

damage (v) 46 have a negative effect on

deafness (n) 73 not being able to hear

decent (adj) 9 not shocking or offensive

decision (n) 19 what you decide to do

defend (v) 17 speak for, say good things about

degree (n) 35 university qualification

delay (v) 46 make slower, make late

demonstrate (v) 62 show

denim (n) 44 cloth (usually blue or black) that jeans are made of

destroy (v) 58 eliminate, break, kill, get rid of

destruction (n) 60 destroying

details (n) 27 specific information

detention (n) 33 punishment of keeping a pupil at school after school hours

detergent (n) 82 chemical product (not soap) used for cleaning, especially clothes

device (n) 71 small piece of equipment

dialect (n) 67 different form of a language, used in one place or part of a country

diet (n) 18 eating less food or special food in order to lose weight

dilemma (n) 75 very difficult choice

diplomacy (n) 66 relations with other countries (with ambassadors, consuls etc.)

disability (n) 7 not being able to do something (eg. see, hear, walk)

disabled (adj) 6 not able to use your body in the normal way

disapprove (v) 64 have a bad opinion (of someone/ something, for moral reasons)

disaster (n) 60 something terrible

disastrous (adj) 58 terrible

discreet (adj) 30 sensible

disease (n) 10 illness

distrust (v) 86 consider dishonest

document (n) 72 letter, report etc. (on paper/a computer)

documentary (n) 48 TV programme about society, history or the environment

dramatic (adj) 59 very big, very fast etc. [adv = **dramatically**]

drop out of (phr v) 85 leave (school, college) before you have finished

duckling (n) 18 baby duck

dye (v) 20 change the colour of

 E

effective (adj) 7 successful

element (n) 66 part of a situation/problem

emotional (adj) 38 strong (feelings)

encouragement (n) 21 words which give courage and confidence

end of the line (np, coll) 72 situation when you cannot continue/make progress

enormous (adj) 67 very big

environment (n) 58 the air/ land/water around us [adj = **environmental**]

essential (adj) 11 necessary, most important

establish (v) 83 build

established (adj) 14 old, well-known

estimated (adj) 74 approximate

ethnic (adj) 44 from a different racial group/ country (eg. ethnic music, fashion, food)

ethnic group (np) 81 race, type of people (eg. Asian, Jewish, white, black)

eventually (adv) 70 finally, in the end

evidence (*n*) 23 information about a crime, from a scientific study

evolution (*n*) 24 scientific idea, first explained by Charles Darwin, that plants and animals have gradually developed since time began

exclude (*v*) 19 leave out, not invite

excursion (*n*) 33 trip, day out

excusable (*adj*) 63 forgivable

execution (*n*) 28 killing a criminal (eg. in the electric chair)

exhibition (*n*) 14 collection of paintings/photos etc. which you can visit

expect (*v*) 28 think something is going to happen

expectations (*n*) 83 strong hopes (about life, relationships)

expel (*v*) 32 send away from school

experiment (*v*) 15 try something new

exploit (*v*) 7 use a person without helping him/her

exposure (*n*) 46 being given/shown something, experiencing something

expulsion (*n*) 33 the most serious school punishment: sending a pupil away from school for ever

extinct (*adj*) 61 not existing any more (eg. dinosaurs)

extinction (*n*) 12 being/ becoming extinct

F

faith (*n*) 24 belief, religion

family background (*np*) 19 your family situation (social, racial, financial etc.)

fare (*n*) 64 the cost of a bus or train ticket

fatal (*adj*) 90 resulting in death

feature (*v*) 9 show, contain

feed (*v*) 74 give food to

firing squad (*np*) 29 the police or soldiers who shoot and kill a criminal in an execution

fixed (*adj*) 27 unchangeable, stuck

flesh (*n*) 50 meat

flexible (*adj*) 89 easy to change; 91 able to move easily

force (*v*) 18 make yourself/ someone do something which you/they don't want to

forearm (*n*) 6 the arm below the elbow

forgive (*v*) 28 stop being angry with someone after s/he has done something wrong

G

generation (*n*) 84 people of the same age

genuinely (*adv*) 86 really

get on (*phr v*) 6 try to do well

get on with (*phr v*) 54 be friends with

glamorous (*adj*) 13 attractive, beautiful

goggles (*n*) 91 equipment to protect the eyes

gorgeous (*adj*) 57 beautiful

graffiti (*n*) 16 writing or drawings (usually political or rude) done on public walls

guaranteed (*adj*) 14 definite, certain

guilty (*adj*) 26 criminally responsible; 86 feeling you have done something wrong

H

habit (*n*) 52 doing something regularly without thinking (eg. smoking is a bad habit)

hand ... into (*v*) 62 take to the right place (eg. the police station)

hang (*v*) 29 execute a criminal with a rope around the neck

hypocrisy (*n*) 80 pretending to believe something

I

identity (*n*) 79 who you are

illegal (*adj*) 35 not legal; against the law

image (*n*) 6 the way people see you; 21 picture (on a page or on film/TV)

immoral (*adj*) 13 bad, wrong

impress (*v*) 86 show people you are clever, good etc.

incident (*n*) 81 something unusual which happens (eg. an accident, a fight)

indignant (*adj*) 50 angry

individual (*n*) 59 one person (not a company or the government)

inequality (*n*) 86 not being equal, not having the same opportunities etc.

inferior to (*adj*) 88 worse than

influence (*n*) 42 power to change

inject (*v*) 29 put into your body with a syringe

instrument (*n*) 66 something useful

insult (*n*) 21 a way of being rude and offensive

integrate (*v*) 81 mix with other people, give up your own culture

intense (*adj*) 38 very strong

interpreting (*n*) 69 spoken translating

invisible (*adj*) 74 who/which cannot be seen

involve (*v*) 11 need, require

J

jogging (*n*) 93 running slowly for exercise

joke (*n*) 14 a funny story or action

judge (*v*) 86 consider good/bad

WORDLIST

L

lead a life (*vp*) 70   live

leading (*adj*) 46   top, most important

legal (*adj*) 9   allowed by the law

lethal (*adj*) 29   something which kills

life-style (*n*) 48   how you live, your culture

lifelong (*adj*) 54   continuing right through your life

limb (*n*) 6   arm or leg

limited (*adj*) 34   small

linguistic (*adj*) 66   connected to language

local (*adj*) 66   in a certain area [**local football team** = the team that plays for that town/village/area]

M

major (*adj*) 14   big, important, famous

make contact with (*vp*) 83   telephone or write (to)

make inquiries (*vp*) 18   ask

material (*n*) 45   what something is made of (eg. cotton/silk/ leather)

maternity leave (*np*) 89   when a woman doesn't work because she is going to have a baby

mature (*adj*) 82   acting or looking older than your age

means (*n*) 59   way/method of transport (eg. train, bus, tram, car)

media (*n*) 15   different ways of doing art (eg. painting, drawing, sculpture etc.); 42   newspapers/radio/TV

mentally (*adv*) 22   in your mind

messy (*adj*) 54   dirty, untidy

middle-class (*adj*) 46   quite rich

minor (*adj*) 66   small, less important or famous

miracle (*n*) 18   surprising, wonderful event

mobility (*n*) 73   ability to move

multi-cultural (*adj*) 25   society with many cultures and different types of people

N

nature (*n*) 55   character

nowadays (*adv*) 43   these days, now

nuisance (*n*) 50   an annoying problem

O

obscene (*adj*) 10   very offensive; disgusting

observe (*v*) 86   say, make a comment

obsessed (*adj*) 43   always thinking about the same thing; too interested in one thing only

obstacle (*n*) 80   problem which stops you

offend (*v*) 7   make ... angry, embarrassed, disgusted [*adj*: **offensive**]

officially (*adv*) 22   in public and formally

oppose (*v*) 10   try to stop; say no to something

option (*n*) 50   choice

originality (*n*) 45   being unusual or different

outfit (*n*) 45   set of clothes

outrageous (*adj*) 44   wild, crazy, unusual

overcome (*v*) 81   deal with (problems/difficulties)

overweight (*adj*) 52   too heavy

P

paramedic (*n*) 36   someone who works with doctors (eg. nurses, ambulance people etc.)

participate (*v*) 23   take part, join in

passive (*adj*) 7   not active, doing nothing

pathetic (*adj*) 56   helpless, stupid

paw (*n*) 12   animal's foot

penalty (*n*) 28   punishment

perm (*n*) 20   [abbreviation for **permanent wave**] a way of curling hair using chemicals

personality (*n*) 19   character (eg. strong, weak)

pesticide (*n*) 61   chemical for killing bad insects etc.

physically (*adv*) 21   connected with the body

pierce (*v*) 20   make a hole in (ears, nose etc. for jewellery)

pinpoint (*v*) 38   say exactly

pitch (*n*) 93   field where sport is played

plastic surgery (*np*) 20   method of repairing/changing parts of the body using skin or bone taken from other parts of the body

poacher (*n*) 12   person who hunts animals or fishes illegally

pocket (*v*) 62   take and keep something dishonestly (to put in your pocket)

pocket money (*np*) 36   money which parents give to children to spend

poetic (*adj*) 67   like in a poem

pointless (*adj*) 7   having no meaning

popular (*adj*) 9   liked by many people

positive (*adj*) 6   hopeful, good

potential (*adj*) 10   possible

powerful (*adj*) 38   strong

pregnant (*adj*) 58   going to have a baby

prematurely (*adv*) 10   before the normal time

presence (*n*) 74   existence, being in a place

present (*adj*) 78   in this/that place

preserve (*v*) 14   keep; 61   not give up

pressure (*n*) 83   problems, difficulties (eg. at work or at home)

preventable (*adj*) 77 can be avoided, stopped

product (*n*) 7 something made by people; something you can buy in the shops

profit (*v*) 66 get money or something good as a result

prolonged (*adj*) 90 lasting a long time

protein (*n*) 50 substance in food like meat, fish, eggs, milk and beans

protesters (*n*) 10 group of people who are politically/ morally against something

provide (*v*) 42 give

puff (*n*) 36 smoking a cigarette for a moment

R

racism (*n*) 78 feelings or actions against other races

reaction (*n*) 11 how you feel about something that happens

reasonable (*adj*) 30 acceptable, sensible

reassure (*v*) 18 make ... feel happier

rebellious (*adj*) 22 fighting against the rules

recall (*v*) 50 remember

reconstruct (*v*) 10 build again

reduce (*v*) 26 make smaller

reference materials (*np*) 73 dictionaries, encyclopaedias etc.

regime (*n*) 81 government

regional (*adj*) 67 in regions/parts of a country

reincarnation (*n*) 24 after dying, your soul comes back in a different body

relationship (*n*) 38 close friendship

release (*v*) 26 let go, let free (eg. from prison)

remain (*v*) 61 still exist, be left

remove (*v*) 18 take out/off

repeatedly (*adv*) 26 again and again

report (*v*) 50 say: 63 tell somebody in authority (eg. a teacher, police officer)

representative (*n*) 33 person who has been chosen to speak and act for others in a group

reproduce (*v*) 51 have babies

research (*n*) 10 study, work of a scientist or academic person

resistance (*n*) 80 people trying to stop you

respect (*v*) 86 believe that someone/something is good

responsibility (*n*) 30 ability to make good, sensible decisions

restore (*v*) 14 repair

retire (*v*) 92 give up a job because of old age

revenge (*v*) 28 hurt someone because someone has hurt you

revolutionise (*v*) 58 change completely

ridiculous (*adj*) 49 silly, stupid

rise (*n*) 66 increase

risk (*n*) 58 dangerous situation

role (*n*) 77 contribution, position

routine (*n*) 50 doing something regularly

row (*n*) 83 fight, argument

S

scar (*n*) 20 mark on the skin from a cut

scene (*n*) 48 part of a film/TV programme

sentimental value (*np*) 62 important personal/emotional connections

senior (*adj*) 10 important

separate (*v*) 26 break the connection; 40 stop living together

servant (*n*) 89 person who works for you in your home

settle down (*phr v*) 80 get married, buy a house, have children

shame (*n*) 22 bad feeling about yourself because you have done something wrong

shoplift (*v*) 65 steal from a shop

shut up (*phr v*) 78 be quiet, stop talking

sincere (*adj*) 30 speaking the truth, saying what you really feel

skip (*v, coll*) 83 miss on purpose

software (*n*) 79 programs for computers

solidarity (*n*) 86 staying together against an enemy

source (*n*) 90 cause

species (*n*) 60 type of animal or plant

split up (*phr v*) 40 stop living/ working/going out together

spread (*n*) 66 increasing distribution

stamina (*n*) 91 energy and mental strength which allow people to exercise/work for a long time

standard (*n*) 46 level of ability; the way you measure/judge something

stare (*v*) 18 look at for a long time

status symbol (*np*) 44 something which shows a person's class or money

strain (*n*) 90 hurt to the body caused by pulling a muscle

stretch (*v*) 20 make longer

strict (*adj*) 30 making sure that people obey the rules

striking (*adj*) 7 unusual and noticeable

struggle (*n*) 67 fight, argument

stylish (*adj*) 7 fashionable, well designed

suffer from (*v*) 50 have (illness/disease)

suicide (*n*) 77 killing yourself

suitable (*adj*) 26 acceptable

superior (to) (*adj*) 86 better (than)

superstitious (*adj*) 24 believing in old ideas about luck and magic

support (*v*) 21 show to be true; 70 help

WORDLIST

survey (*n*) 34 set of questions to find out public opinions

suspension (*n*) 33 punishment of not allowing a pupil to come to school for a few days/weeks

switch (*v*) 68 changing between two things

synthesizer (*n*) 73 computer that makes music or speech

take ... seriously (*v*) 86 give a lot of attention to

taste (*n*) 6 ideas about what is good and bad (eg. in art, music, fashion, style)

tattoo (*n*) 20 picture on the skin done with a needle and ink

tetanus (*n*) 77 serious bacterial disease

theft (*n*) 27 stealing, crime done by a thief

thought-provoking (*adj*) 7 making people think

threaten (*v*) 13 promise something bad

timid (*adj*) 54 shy, not confident

tiny (*adj*) 61 very small

tolerate (*v*) 30 accept, not mind

touching (*adj*) 7 making people feel sympathetic

trade (*n*) 66 buying and selling

trade union (*np*) 89 organisation of workers/ employees which talks to employers about pay etc.

train (*v*) 13 teach an animal or person to do something; 90 exercising the body

training (*n*) 89 learning new skills for work

trap (*n*) 12 thing to catch animals

treat (*v*) 18 how to behave with someone (well, badly etc.); 28 give medical help

treatment (*n*) 10 way of curing a disease

trust (*v*) 30 feel that someone has good intentions

umbilical cord (*np*) 77 cord which joins mother and baby together when the baby is born

underweight (*adj*) 42 too light

unemployed (*adj*) 62 not having a job

unfairly (*adv*) 18 not correctly

uniform (*n*) 78 set of clothes worn by everyone in a particular group/job (eg. the police)

upset (*adj*) 55 sad, unhappy

useless (*adj*) 86 not good (≠ useful)

vaccine (*n*) 76 medicine (usually an injection) which protects you from a virus

valuable (*adj*) 55 good; 63 expensive

van (*n*) 78 type of car for transporting goods

vandalize (*v*) 14 damage/break something only for fun

victim (*n*) 6 someone who suffers because of illness, bad luck or another person's actions

view (*n*) 8 opinion, what you think about something

viewer (*n*) 49 someone who watches TV

violence (*n*) 48 hitting, shooting, killing etc.

vision (*n*) 23 religious experience when God or a saint appears

volunteer (*v*) 82 give information without being asked

warning sign (*np*) 50 sign of a problem in the near future

wax (*v*) 20 remove hair from the body

whole grain (*np*) 50 cereals (eg. wheat and rice) which have not been processed

wildlife reserve (*np*) 58 park for wild, free animals

working out (*np*) 93 taking physical exercise

worldwide (*adv*) 23 all over the world

wrist (*n*) 78 part of the body (between the arm and the hand)

yoga (*n*) 24 Hindu philosophy which teaches control of the mind and body

youth club (*np*) 18 place where there are activities for young people

Z

zinc (*n*) 50 metal which we should eat in very small quantities as part of a healthy diet